Inner Mysteries of the Goths

Rune-Lore & Secret Wisdom of the Northern Tradition

By Nigel Pennick

D1270543

Inner Mysteries of the Goths
Rune-Lore & Secret Wisdom of the Northern Tradition

©1995 Nigel Pennick

ISBN 1 898307 51 2

Cover design by Daryth Bastin
Cover illustration by Nigel Pennick

Published by:

Capall Bann Publishing
Freshfields
Chieveley
Berks
RG20 8TF

Tel/Fax 01635 248711

Contents

By the same author, also published by Capall Bann:

Sacred Geometry
Oracle of Geomancy
Signs, Symbols and Sigils
Runic Astrology
The Goddess Year (with Helen Field)

Introduction

This is a book about the runes used by the ancient Goths, and their unique alphabet, which, derived from the runes, is also used as a system of divination. Although a lot has been written about the runes, there is still more to say, because, since they became popular again after the 1960s, they have developed and continue to flourish and enter new areas unheard of by their practitioners of ancient days.

The use of runes as an oracle is meaningless unless it exists as a living tradition, which means that its primary function is to be something that is practised. Practice means that inherent within the system exists a degree of flexibility and intuitive development that resembles to a greater degree the way that oral, pre-literate societies transmitted their knowledge. Today, this magical current does not possess exactly the same character as older, pre-literate, oral traditions, which, of course, it cannot. However, we would be mistaken in imagining that everything done with regard to the Northern Tradition is identical to the prescriptions found in books.

---

1. The Latin motto *Lux e Tenebris* - "From out of the Shadows, Light" - here rendered in the Gothic alphabet, is emblematical of the coming-into-being, or creation, of existence. All religious systems have a creation-myth which in some way or other manifests this concept. Because illumination of the individual is a microcosmic reflection of the formation of matter out of nothingness, the great work of self-enlightenment is a means for each of us to come into a state of oneness with the all.

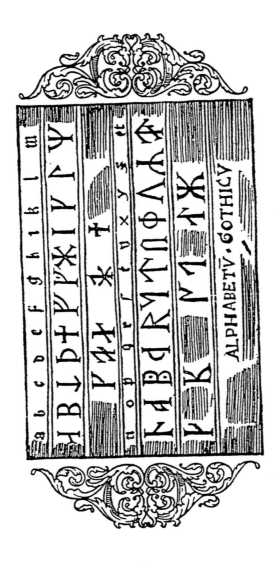

2. The *Alphabetum Gothicum*, from Olaus Magnus. This was the final version of the runes, used in Sweden until the 18th century, and Estonia until the 20th. Its ultimate origin among the Heruli, a branch of the Goths that originated in what is now Denmark, is recognized by its name.

2

With the Gothic alphabet, as perhaps with the runes, there was a 'proper original', created new by an actual individual. Thus, each character possessed an individual meaning that emanated partly from the spirit of the age, partly from the conscious and subconscious of the man who created the alphabets, and partly from that realm of spirit that is as undefinable as the many words by which it is described. But, immediately Odin or Ulfila let go their creations into the world, other individuals provided their own ways, usages and interpretations. Thus the process of örlog added and altered the systems, through changing times and equally changing needs. Now, in this book, published 1400 years after the Roman Catholic church suppressed the Gothic Alphabet, the Gothic staves are described again along with their runic siblings as a system of seership.

Among other human activities, divination is an intensely personal practice. Whenever a divination is conducted, the essentials of each performance remain unchanged, but each one that we perform is in essence something new, which partakes of the unique quality of the time and place it is performed and the people who are doing it.

Essentially, when we divine, we are doing something that has never been done before. We recreate the system every time we use it, for it has no existence outside its users. Although the individual characters or runes have specific meanings, Gothic divination has no overall ruling text.

The Chinese *I Ching*, for example, uses a fixed text to interpret specific figures generated in that divinatory system. Also, 'texts' exist as oral stanzas within West African divination, such as Ifa and the Sixteen Cowries. Some of these, too, have been written down and fixed by those who recorded them. However, the Germanic alphabets, as well as Greek and Hebrew used in divination, only have individual meanings, associations and kennings that indicate the meaning of any divination without giving it a fixed, textual, association. This flexibility and freedom within an agreed framework provides us with a powerful tool to investigate every area of human experience from an otherworldly perspective. This is the power that divination gives us. It is up to use to use it wisely, for the good of all.

Nigel Pennick,
Bar Hill,
Spring Equinox 1995 ce.

Chapter 1
The Background of Gothic Divination

The Goths

The earliest known homeland of the people known as the Goths was in southern Scandinavia, where they pursued a mixed economy of agriculture, gathering and hunting. The Gothic people had a culture in common with other northern European peoples, and spoke a language later classified as part of the East Germanic group. To this day, the large Baltic island to the east of modern Sweden, Gotland, bears their name and relics of their culture. It appears that around the beginning of the common era, the pressures of an increasing population led the Goths to undertake a mass emigration from Scandinavia, across the Baltic to the shores of mainland Europe, to the valley of the River Vistula in what is now Poland. Gothic legend tells that, led by king Filimer, they sailed in only three ships.

From the Vistula region, in the second century of the Common Era, under their fifth king, with a continual increase in population, the Goths decided to migrate eastwards. The Goths appear to have been a federation of a number of different tribes. The earliest recorded grouping of the Goths was known as the Greuthingi. Another significant branch of the nation was the Heruli, originally from northern Denmark, whose name later became synonymous with runemasters. But, in their migrations eastwards, the Gothic nation became divided into two separate groups. Jordanes, the Gothic historian, recounts how the eastward-moving Gothic nation was crossing the great river Dnieper on a bridge at the place which later became Kiev. After about half of the enormous throng of wagons, horses, livestock and people had crossed over, the bridge broke down, and the Goths were split between those who had crossed to the east bank and those left behind on the west. Because they did not have the knowledge or ability to reconstruct the bridge, the Goths were effectively divided into two groups. Those who had crossed were called the eastern Goths - the Ostrogoths - and those left behind became the western Goths - the Visigoths.

The Ostrogoths - those who had crossed the River Dnieper - continued their eastward trek towards the Donets, then invaded the Crimea, where some settled. In the Ukraine, the Cherniakhov civilization may have actually come into being as the result of a fusion between Gothic and local people. Other parts of the Gothic nation continued their expansion across the Cimmerian Bosphorus and into the valley of Kuban. West of the Dnieper, the Visigoths travelled southwards to the Black Sea, conquering the coastal regions as far as the Danube. Here, they took over the Greek Kingdom of the Bosphorus, which had existed for several centuries as a complex multi-ethnic trading nation that had business dealings with the local Roxolani, Sarmatians and Scythians. Bosphoran businessmen were the major regional dealers in wine, jewelry, ceramics, metalwork and swords, buying and selling Sarmatian, Turkic, Roman and Germanic products. Through these pluralistic connections, the Goths gradually evolved a synthesis between the Germanic barbarian culture and the classical tradition of the Greeks. Such are the roots of current European civilization.

By the middle of the third century, the whole northern coast of the Black Sea was under Gothic rule. At that time, both the Ostrogoths and Visigoths were respected and feared as formidable warlike nations whose prowess had been proven by their conquests. Then, the Ostrogothic realms stretched across a vast territory, from the Don to the Dniester, from the Black Sea to Belarus. Also having consolidated their conquests, the Visigoths sent expeditionary armies, strengthened by Sarmatian cavalry, to mount successive raiding adventures into Roman territory across the Danube. In the year 251 the Roman Emperor, Decius, attempted to halt the Visigoths' attacks once and for all. But instead of eliminating the Goths, his Roman army was defeated decisively, and the Emperor slain. In the subsequent onslaught of the Visigoths against the Empire, many cities and towns were laid waste, but the Greek cities of Panticapaeum and Olbia were spared to serve as bases for further attacks against the Romans. Also, after the defeat of Decius's army, an Ostrogothic fleet sailed from Kerch to attack the southern shore of the Black Sea. The seaborne army sacked the city of Trebizond and finally returned to the north shore laden with booty and slaves. Subsequently, Gothic fleets regularly harried the maritime provinces of the Eastern Roman (Byzantine) Empire, sailing through the Dardanelles to attack islands in the Aegean in the manner of the later Vikings.

In the year 267, the Heruli, still a distinct sub-element of the Goths, mounted an assault against Athens, and despite fierce resistance under Herennus Dexippus, sacked the city, looted the shrines and made a bonfire of many books. However, and paradoxically, the Heruli were also instrumental in spreading the runes, which one of their priests may have developed from elements of the Greek or North Italic alphabets. Although the Heruli were finally defeated and scattered, the name Erilaz (Herulian) became the title of a runemaster in places where the runes were used. It is still used today as a generic term for a contemporary runemaster-priest or runemistress-priestess, though it is impossible today for anyone to trace their descent with any certainty from an ethnic Herulian.

In the first half of the fourth century, the Gothic leaders reluctantly adopted the Arian version of the Christian religion, which was soon to be declared unorthodox and heretical by the triumphant Trinitarians. Ulfila, the first bishop and founder of the Gothic Church, translated a version of the New Testament into the Gothic language, which he wrote in a new alphabet of his invention. This Gothic alphabet cleverly combined elements of the Gothic Runic futhark and the Greek alphabet, creating something new. It is this mystical alphabet that is detailed later in this book. As with all of the many incursions of the Christian religion into Pagan Europe, conversion was slow and incomplete, with frequent setbacks and reverses. Also, during conversion, not all Pagan elements were extirpated. Throughout Europe, whenever Christian belief and practice were imposed, many Pagan cultural elements were retained. Inevitably, this created a twofold religion, sometimes called a 'dual faith'. One side of European Christianity preached gospel orthodoxy, whilst the other side continued to practise Pagan ceremonies under the aegis of Christian festivals. Before protestant puritanism was invented in the sixteenth century, this was the normal way that religion was conducted in so-called Christendom.

In the middle of the fourth century, the Ostrogoths elected Ermerich as king. Under his rule, the area of Gothic power expanded still further, and the ancient Greek Kingdom of the Bosphorus was overrun finally. His armies crossed the Dnieper and occupied the west bank. Then they advanced to the upper Vistula, and raided the lands of the Balts. Finally, as all hero-kings should, Ermenric died in battle against the Huns. At his death, the Ostrogothic kingdom stretched from the Baltic to the Black sea, and from the Kuban to the Dniester and the Vistula. But around 375, the territory of the Ostrogoths was invaded by the Huns. The Gothic kingdom was no match for this terrifying mobile warrior-nation, and the migrations began anew. The Goths were forced westwards, though not all left their territories, and not all influence was destroyed, for the Gothic language was spoken in the Crimea until around 1554. The Ostrogoths played a significant role in the decisive battle fought by the barbarians in the year 378 against the

Romans at Adrianople, 150 miles north-west of Constantinople. There, the Emperor Valens, his generals and 40,000 Roman troops were massacred.

Despite this great victory against the Empire, after the Ostrogoths' defeat at the hands of the Huns, between 382 and 395, Arian Christianity was adopted more widely by the Goths. As the western Roman Empire disintegrated into chaos, the Goths attempted to break through into the eastern half. The process was resisted strongly by Roman forces, which had been reconstructed since the reverse at Adrianople. In the year 386, the Ostrogoths under their general, Odotheus, attempted to cross the Danube on rafts, but were destroyed in midstream by the forces of the Roman general Promotus, and the river was choked with corpses of the slain. But in 395 the Goths under Alaric fought their way into Greece, destroying and looting Pagan sanctuaries. Later, in 401, they moved into Italy, but were driven out by the forces of the Roman general Stilicho. Other Gothic invasions took the Visigoths to southern Gaul (later France) and Iberia.

During this process, Gothic warriors fought on both the Roman and Barbarian sides. Some were mercenaries or *foederati* of the Roman forces, whilst others fought for their own booty in the Gothic forces. The Roman army that in 394 defeated Eugenius, Pagan emperor of the West, contained Gothic mercenaries under the command of Alaric. In 405, led by a Scythian Pagan called Radegais, a force of over 200,000 Goths invaded Italy, but were defeated by Alaric's Gothic forces. But the end of Roman power was near, for in 408 Alaric set up Attalus as puppet emperor in the west. The disintegration of the western Roman Empire continued, with the Emperors at Constantinople trying almost vainly to restore order against impossible odds. On August 24, 410, the holy city of Rome, believed by most to be invincible, fell to the Gothic army of Alaric. The whole city was sacked, and only the sanctuary of St Peter, on Cybele's sacred hill, the Vatican, was spared. In 414, Ataulf succeeded Alaric as king, but he was assassinated in

415. For years, almost continuous warfare raged over the remains of the western Empire, with subsequent mixing of peoples and cultures.

In 455, the forces of the Vandals, under Genseric, took Rome, and in 476, the last Emperor of the West, Romulus Augustulus, was deposed by Odoacer, leader of the Heruli, who occupied Sicily, formerly held by the Vandals. In the year 493, Odoacer was in turn overthrown by an Ostrogoth, Theodoric the Great, who assumed power in Italy with the authorisation of the eastern Emperor, Zeno, and ruled from the former western imperial capital of Ravenna. After his death, Theodoric was apotheosized in the tradition of Germanic kingship. His mausoleum, which still exists, is a remarkable ten-sided structure that demonstrates the technical skill and symbolic knowledge of its architect and the masons who built it. Theodoric became celebrated in Germanic legend as having being sired by a divine father, of having possessed the ability to breathe fire like a dragon, and, after his death, appearing on earth sometimes as a shade leading the Wild Hunt along the Rhine. In this way, Theodoric was celebrated far away from Italy, in the Gothic ancestral homelands. The celebrated ninth century runestone at Rök in Sweden invokes Theodoric, who is "mounted ready on his horse, with his shield strapped on".

After an age of decline and disintegration, the Roman Empire in the west of mainland Europe broke up and stabilised into new territories: What later became northern and central France was ruled by Frankish and Burgundian kings. Italy was under the Ostrogoths, whilst the Visigoths ruled from Gibraltar to the Loire, having conquered the territory between 509 and 531. The former Roman provinces of North Africa were ruled for a while by another celebrated barbarian nation, the Vandals, until they were overthrown by the power of Constantinople in 533. Like that of the Vandals, the power of the Goths was not enduring. Ostrogothic power was broken in 555 by the forces of the Eastern Roman Empire in a concerted campaign to re-conquer Italy. In Iberia, the Visigothic kingdom was overrun by Moslem Arab and Berber forces after the year 711, and what survived of the Visigothic nobility was taken prisoner and carried in triumph to Damascus where they were killed or enslaved. Destroyed by Byzantine and Islamic armed force, the Goths were dispersed and ceased to retain an ethnic identity. Because of this, the Gothic tradition has become obscure, and the Gothic alphabet has received less attention than is its due. Later commentators, especially in the 18th century, associated the Goths with barbarousness, and gave their name to the form of medieval architecture that is characterised by pointed arches, which they saw as inferior to the Classical system of building. In the 19th century, the term Gothic became applied to a genre of romantic literature that also had no real connection with the ancient ethnic nation. Today the ancient Goths have no modern state that can elevate them to the status of ancestral heroes, as the Republic of Ireland does the ancient Celts, or Israel the ancient Jews. Whether this is a good thing or a bad thing is a matter of debate.

Gothic Religion

The Goths practised a form of Paganism well known in northern Europe. Although there are few records, it seems that Gothic beliefs and practices contained elements of both of the traditions we know well from Scandinavia at the end of the first millennium. Gothic religion expressed elements of the Vanic tradition that revered the earth mother Nerthus and the phallic generative god, Freyr, and also elements of the Ansic tradition, represented by deities that parallel the better-known Germanic pantheon of Tîwaz, Woden, Thor etc. According to contemporary accounts, the Goths are said to have worshipped Mars, hanging spoils of war on sacred tree trunks dedicated to him. In 1837, a hoard known as 'The Treasure of the Goths' was discovered at Pietroasa (in modern Rumania). Probably buried during an attack by the Huns in 376, it was composed entirely of gold vases, cups and sacred artifacts. It is clear that

3. Pagan Gothic oath-ring discovered at Pietroasa in Rumania. It bears
a runic inscription honouring Jupiter, god of the Goths.

the treasure belonged to a Pagan sanctuary, for among the holy objects was an altar- or oath-ring that weighed 25 ounces (700 grams). It bore the inscription, in runes, GUTAN IOWI HAILAG. The meaning of this inscription is disputed, though it appears to be the straightforward dedication "To Jove (Jupiter), God of the Goths". It is likely that the *interpretation Romana* was working here, with the Germanic god-names being rendered by the Goths themselves according to their classical parallels. Thus, the worship of Mars can be seen as the Romanised Tîwaz (Tyr) and Jove as Thor.

Oath-rings like this were a characteristic element of the temples dedicated to Thor in Scandinavia, Iceland and Ireland, and so the dedication of the ring to Jupiter is perfectly in keeping with that tradition. Contemporary descriptions of the ancient temples of Thor, tell how heavy arm-rings of iron or gold lay on the altars. Oaths were taken upon 'the holy armlet of Thor', which only the priest wore during religious rituals. After Arian Christianity was adopted, the Gothic priests continued the Pagan tradition of wearing arm-rings as part of their regalia. Gothic Pagan burials are characterised by a relative rarity of weapons, compared with those from other Germanic traditions, but why this should be so is a matter of speculation.

As Thunor, the Saxons worshipped the thunder god in special *temenoi*, sacred clearings in the woodland, in which stood holy oak trees. All over Europe, the oak is the tree of the thunder god. In northern Europe, it is the tree of Thor and Taranis. In southern Europe, it is sacred to Zeus and Jupiter, and in the Baltic region, to Perkunas. Oak trees that have been struck by lightning are especially revered, having been blessed by the god.

It is likely that the Gothic *xoana* of the god Thor/Jupiter were made of oak trees, perhaps archaic ones formerly revered when they were standing. Mobile images were necessary for a travelling nation like the Goths. The image of Thor at

4. The trinity of Scandinavian deities. Left: Frigg; centre, enthroned: Thor, and right, Tyr or Odin. The interpretation of the gods, as with all free systems, is open to individual choice. Engraving from the works of Olaus Magnus.

Thrandheim, in Iceland, for example, recorded in *Flateyjarbók*, was mobile, being placed in a wheeled chariot bedecked by silver and gold and pulled by images of goats.

According to Jordanes, the Visigoths regarded their past leaders as deified beings, called the Anses. They were elevated to the pantheon because, through their power, we are told, their living descendants were inspired towards victory in battle. Thus, Ammianus tells us that the Visigothic warriors went into battle "shouting the praises of their ancestors". Ancestor-veneration among the Goths is not an unusual practice, for it is a characteristic element of European Paganism in general. The ancestor as god is an integral element of the elder faith, appearing in many different ways throughout history. The Celtic nobility were descended from the god Beli and the goddess Anna. To this day, the English monarch and German nobility count their descent from the ancestral deity Woden, whilst under State Paganism, Roman emperors were officially deified after their death. The Gothic rune and word **ansuz*, meaning a sovereign deity, is cognate with the Norse name for the gods of order and progress, the Aesir. In the Norse context, it seems to denote apotheosized human ancestors. We have evidence for this from the Icelandic historian, Snorri Sturluson, who, in his *Heimskringla*, tells the story of a great king of the Alans called Odin (Woden), who lived in what is now southern Russia, and who, through migrations of his folk, had significant influence on various parts of Europe. Similarly, among others the architect Imhotep, the poet Homer, the philosopher Pythagoras, the geometer Petosiris, the Emperor Alexander and the prophet Jesus of Nazareth, were elevated to the status of god by their devotees after their deaths.

Little is known about the Gothic sacred year, mainly because virtually all Gothic writings were burnt in Spain in 589 by order of the Catholic Church. The only uniquely Gothic religious festival now known comes from a fragment of a Christian calendar that mentions the celebration of Fruma

5. Gothic Pagan images or *xoana* being paraded on camels. Image from a triumphal column formerly at Constantinople, from *Imperium Orientale* by A. Banduri, Venice, 1729.

Jiuleis, "The First Yule" in November. Unfortunately, this tantalising glimpse is all we have of what was once undoubtedly a comprehensive Gothic Pagan calendar.

Contact with the rich ferment of religions that was occurring in the Roman Empire led devotees of the proselytising Christian cults to travel into the lands of the Goths. There, they attempted to convince Pagans to give up their ancestral heritage and instead take up their beliefs and practices. The Bishop Ulfila, a follower of the Arian variant of Christianity, was successful in converting a proportion of Goths to his religion. This ewas largely because Ulfila devised an alphabet based on Greek and Runic in which he wrote his own translation of the Greek New Testament in the Gothic language. Through this text, Ulfila was able to convert some of the Goths from their Pagan beliefs and practices. But Gothic Christianity, like the other versions of the religion practised at that time, bears little resemblance to the multiple Christian sects that proliferate in the late 20th century, all claiming, counter to common sense, that they are the one true version. The Goths developed a syncretic religion in which the Arian version of Christianity was deconstructed and then re-interpreted according to a Pagan structure. As in the Trinitarian churches, Pagan elements continued to play an important role in the newer practices.

The Orthodox church historian Socrates records that between 369 and 372, the Goths resisted incursions of Orthodox and Arian Christianity because "the ancestral religion was being debased". To cleanse the soil and thereby re-consecrate the land, Athaneric ordered a *xoanon* to be carried on a wagon around each settlement. They were to be taken to the homes of those suspected of being Christians, who then were required to partake of the sacred food served at ceremonies in honour of the gods. The *xoana* were images, rather like the Greek herm, a carved representation of human head, usually that of Hermes (Mercury, Woden), atop a pillar or post. Elsewhere in European Pagan tradition, similar sacred images are known among the Celts and Lapps. An illustration of the Gothic images, carried on camels, was carved on a triumphal column at Constantinople. An engraving of it is reproduced here. The mausoleum of the Arian Christian king Theodoric at Ravenna was once surrounded by pillars which may have been stone successors of the wooden sacred images of the Goths.

In his attempt to eliminate foreign elements from Gothic society, king Athaneric ordered that Christians of whatever sect must partake of the sacred communal meal in each community where they lived. It was a reasonable test of loyalty to clan and nation. Any member of Gothic society who refused to partake of the ceremonial meal automatically dissociated himself or herself from the life of the clan. By refusing to participate in religious ceremonies, the objector also absented him- or herself from social duties and rights, becoming at once an outcast, legally dead. When Athaneric imposed this test of loyalty, Ulfila, and many other Gothic Christians, fled into non-Gothic lands where they could live without being compelled to demonstrate their allegiance. Ulfila hid out in Moesia. He died around the year 382. But in 372, the Orthodox Christian fanatic, Saba, later canonized as a saint, refused to share in a common meal, as demanded by law. As he had disgraced himself in the eyes of the community, he was allowed to go away. But instead of staying away, and doing something else with his life, he returned later, and the same thing happened again. Finally, after refusing for a third time to conform to the norms of society, he was arrested once more. Even then, the authorities offered to set him free, so long as he went away and stopped pestering them, but instead, he insisted that his captors should do their duty and kill him. So they did, drowning him in a river. Later, Saba's body was shipped to Cappadocia as a relic, and Saba was admired and worshipped there as a model of Orthodox Christian virtue.

Despite Athaneric's resistance to deculturalisation, the Gothic nobility finally became Arians because it was politically expedient to do so. But Pagan traditions and practices were

18

not abolished. For example, Alaric, conqueror of Rome, was interred according to a non-Christian custom. Completely contrary to all accepted Christian rites of burial, he was entombed in the bed of the River Basentus in southern Italy. Engineers diverted the river into a new channel, and constructed the stone tomb, in which the king's body was sealed. Then, the tomb was completed, and the river was allowed to flow once more in its original bed, enclosing the sepulchre beneath the running waters. Those who had taken part in the burial ceremony were then ritually slain. In England, according to local lore, the Anglian King Offa of Mercia is said to have been buried in a similar manner in the bed of the River Ouse at Bedford. Theodosius was buried in a more conventional manner, but his mausoleum at Ravenna also reflects Pagan tradition, recalling the archaic tradition that the body should be buried above ground level. Made of Istrian stone, the Mausoleum of Theodoric is a regular ten-sided building, containing the king's porphyry sarcophagus on an upper floor. The dome above the sarcophagus has a sunwheel-cross at the centre. It was surrounded by a circle of pillars that reflected the Pagan images of earlier times.

Although Theodosius professed a belief in Arianity, he was nevertheless tolerant in the manner of all enlightened monarchs. His tolerance extended to practitioners of Judaism, as well as the Catholic and Orthodox versions of the Christian religion. As he told the Jews in his Italian kingdom "we cannot impose religion, and no one can be made to believe in spite of himself." Unlike the fundamentalists or fanatics, Theodosius enjoyed hearing theological arguments between different sects and cults. Even members of his own family pleased themselves. His mother, Hereleuwa, was an Orthodox Christian, whilst his daughter, Amalasuintha, was taught by Barbara, a Roman Catholic. Theodosius's Arian church at Ravenna, San Apollinaire Nuovo, which still exists, contained, in classical Pagan tradition, an acknowledgement of the *genius loci*, Felix Ravenna. After the fall of the Gothic kingdom in Italy, the new rulers were less tolerant of pluralistic interpretations of religions. So this church suffered conversion twice. First, the Orthodox hierarchy re-consecrated it according to its rites, and re-named it after St Martin. The fantastic mosaics inside were altered to reflect the new doctrine. Then, in the ninth century, the Catholic Pope Agnellus took it away from the Orthodox religion, and re-dedicated it to St Apollinaris. Ironically, St Apollinaris is himself is a Christian interpretation of the Pagan god Apollo.

The Visigoths finally set up a kingdom in Spain, where Gothic traditions continued until the Islamic conquest. Eured, king of the Visigoths in Spain, resisted all Christian sects that were not Arian, but, in 589, King Reccared suddenly converted from Arianism to Catholicism, and called a Catholic church council at Toledo to enforce his new beliefs on others. This Third Council of Toledo, as it was called officially, set about suppressing Gothic practice. To achieve this, the Arian religion was outlawed, along with many Pagan practices. The elaborate Gothic funerary rites that had continued until then under Arian Christianity were abolished immediately. They had included praise-songs and bane-chants for the dead, and the practice of mourning where men slashed their own chests and those of their kinsmen until they bled on the earth of the grave. Furthermore, all Arian books in the Gothic language and alphabet were heaped on a bonfire. In a single holocaust, much Gothic learning was extirpated for ever. In the same year, a church council held at Narbonne, the ecclesiastics deplored the fact that many Catholics would not work on Thursdays, because it was sacred to Jupiter. For this, free men were punished by being excluded from the church with a year's penance. Slaves who observed Thursdays were to be flogged.

But, as in other parts of Europe, the imposition of the Christian religion of whichever sect was only a superficial change. Cruel sports and punishments, torture, slavery and the death penalty, observed universally by Roman and Barbarian alike, were maintained and sanctioned by the Christian clergy. The mantic arts, once supported by temple hierarchies and official oracle-shrines, were studied now by Christian ecclesiastics and interpreted according to the newer official creed. Classical astrology, geomancy and other forms of divination, proved too valuable to abandon, and so were maintained and modified according to fresh theological interpretations whilst remaining substantially unaltered. Further details of this process can be found in the author's work *The Oracle of Geomancy* (Capall Bann, 1995).

Chapter 2
The Background of Gothic Divination

European Pagan Spirituality

Spiritual ways and techniques have no value at all unless they are manifested here and now in some useful way. If they do not assist human beings in living better, more harmonious and peaceful lives, then they are a sham. At best they are entertainment, and at worst self-delusion or the means for unscrupulous people to dominate others and control them. Sadly, most of the Earth's current spiritual systems ignore the reality of the immediate historical antecedents of the present, and continue to preach as though we are not living in unprecedented times when the Earth has been transformed in ways formerly unimaginable. In the half-century after the apocalypse of the 1940s, the results of that period of intense barbarism are everywhere to see. The processes set in train early in the 20th century are continuing according to their örlog.

That the Earth has some potentially serious ecological problems is an undeniable reality of the present day. But the recognition that its origins in modern industrial civilization have a spiritual basis has yet to emerge on a large scale. Sometimes voices are raised by people from traditional native cultures in countries where immediately recognizable processes, such as the continuing destruction of the rain forests, are taking place. Unfortunately this exploitative aspect of human culture, sometimes presented as a war against Nature is usually presented as being the 'Western' or 'European' way of doing things. But in reality this is no more the European way than any other. Those who blame the Europeans are, through ignorance, wilfulness or political motivation, ignoring the opposite, pre- and para-Christian tradition of nature spirituality, whose roots are in the ancient Paganism of this continent. Unfortunately, the uncaring, triumphalist, dominant attitude towards Nature that seems to be implicit within patriarchal and monotheistic religions is still often wrongly associated with indigenous European tradition.

But the European Pagan view of the world, whether we take the southern or northern versions, is one of harmonious unity. For example, the ancient Greek tradition, which lies at the roots of western civilization, made no distinction between humanity and the natural world. It recognized hat all dividing lines are artificial. The goddesses and gods were seen not as dominators or destroyers of Nature, but as the nurturers and sustainers of the natural order. To the Greeks, the Great God Pan was the guardian of soft streams and thorny thickets, snowy mountains and rocky peaks. According to the Homeric Hymn to Aphrodite, this goddess roused passions in all living things, not just humans, but also "birds that fly in the air, and all of the many beings" of the sea and land. Artemis was worshipped as the mistress of animals. She was viewed as both creator and destroyer, the necessary roles that one must take on if one is to maintain balance. But in one of her most telling myths, she slew the great hunter because he boasted that he would kill all of the animals. To kill more than is necessary, thereby disrupting the ecological balance of the world, is a blasphemous act, which will be punished.

In the mature and balanced viewpoint of the ancient Pagan sages, it is crystal clear that if we choose the road of folly, disrupting the ecosystem of Mother Earth, then we must be prepared to suffer the effects which will come from doing so.

Whether we believe transgressors of natural law have been punished by the gods and goddesses, or whether we interpret it as the natural consequence of cause and effect, the result is the same - ruin and destruction. Nineteen centuries ago, the great and holy Pagan master Apollonius of Tyana expressed this truth thus: "For things that violate Nature can hardly come to be: and in any case, even when they do come into existence, they pass rapidly to destruction". With the present belated realisation that even the robust climatic patterns of our planet have been damaged seriously, and continue to be damaged, by the intemperate activities of human greed, Apollonius's words are ringing true.

In contrast to the Nature-venerating way of European Paganism, the words which have been taken as gospel, serving as the mandate for the triumphalist, uncaring exploitation of the planet can be found in the book called *Genesis* in the Judaeo-Christian *Bible*. In this version of the Middle Eastern creation-myth, the anonymous author tells us that "God said....be fruitful, and multiply, and replenish the earth, and subdue it: and have dominion over the fish of the sea, and over the fowl of the air, and over every living thing that moveth upon the earth". This attitude is in total contrast to the holistic Pagan vision of reality, expressed by the Greek sage Anexagoras, "Nothing exists apart; everything has a share of everything else"(*Fragment* 6). Also, in his *Metaphysics*, Aristotle stated: "All things are ordered together somehow, but they are not all alike, both fishes and fowls and plants; and the world is not such that one thing has nothing to do with another, but they are connected".

Modern technical civilization, whose basic spiritual authorisation is not in the measured wisdom of Anexagoras, Aristotle or Apollonius, but in this Biblical text, generally has turned a blind eye to this reality, though things are changing. To set up the human as separate from Nature is to set up the inevitable future ecological catastrophe, as the natural balance of things reasserts itself, as it inevitably must. This is the underlying truth of Paganism, and the basis for understanding the philosophical background of divinatory alphabets like Greek, Runic and Gothic.

In the Orphic tradition of ancient Greece, for example, the blessed prophet Orpheus emphasised the harmonious interconnectedness of all Nature. The blessed prophet is always depicted surrounded by animals, attracted by his divine song. Orpheus taught that all living beings, human, animal and plant, possess souls and intelligence according to their nature. "The soul inhabits every kind of form in animals in plants" wrote Empedocles. In Nature's original condition, they believed, humans, birds and walking animals had lived in a state of gentleness and peaceful co-existence. Because of this, taught Pythagoras, "to kill living beings is contrary to both custom and nature". Animal sacrifice was abhorred by this current of Pagan thought. Empedocles stated that anyone who sacrificed an animal was "sacrificing his own kinsfolk". Apollonius of Tyana condemned sacrifice and also refused to hunt animals: "It is no pleasure to me to attack animals that have been ill-treated and enslaved in violation of their nature".

The ancient Greek tradition of the followers of Orpheus and Pythagoras, which was related to the Druidic tradition of the Celts to the north, was one of harmony of all organic life. "There is no birth in mortal things", wrote Empedocles, "and no end in ruinous death. There is only a mingling and interchange of parts, and it is this that we call 'Nature'...When these elements are mingled into the shape of a man living under the bright sky, or into the shape of wild beasts or birds, people call it birth; and when these things are separated into their parts, people speak of hapless death". Thus it was that the Orphics and Pythagoreans taught that all life is one, and that this is one with the universe. "I have been a boy and girl, a bush, a bird, and a silent, water-dwelling fish", explained Empedocles. A thousand miles to the north-west, and some centuries later, the British bard Taliesin recounted the same experience. Ultimately, the recognition that all things are inextricably interconnected through space and time is the basis of the creative, Pagan acceptance of life.

Sacrifice, Invocation and Divination

The essential interconnectedness of all aspects of existence means that each part of being contains within it some aspect of the whole. When we gain knowledge of some part of being, then we also gain knowledge of certain aspects of other elements with which it is most intimately linked. By examining Nature, we can understand the workings of the divine, and by working the oracles, we can glimpse the currents of events that are influencing the present and creating the future. In the ancient Northern Tradition, consulting the divine powers through the casting of lots was an important element of decision-making. Tacitus, in his *Germania* refers to a technique which may have been the use of runes marked on slivers of wood taken from fruit-bearing trees. The divine virtue of the tree was thereby utilised in communicating with otherworldly powers. The Norse Pagans, from whom we know the technique, used the divinatory lots, called *Hlaut*, which were carved on special *Hlautviɤr-* (lot-wood). Such a lot-stick was otherwise called *Blotspann*. When the lot was cast, the rite was called *Fella Blotspann*, to let fall the bloodtwig, or *Ganga til frettar*, to institute an enquiry. The diviner's title, *Tyr Hlautarteins*, meant 'lord of the lot-stick'. The lot-stick was closely related to the blood sprinklers called Hlautteinar that were used in sacrificial rites. The Scandinavian *blot* was a sacrifice, celebrated at the sacrificial feast called *blotveizla*, at which some of the ritually-slaughtered animal was eaten in the feasting. As far as can be determined, unlike certain aspects of Greek tradition, the ancient Northern Tradition priesthoods conducted animal sacrifice. Sacrifice of cattle continued under Christian tutelage in the cult of St Beino at Clynnog Fawr in Wales until the 19th century.

26

Sacrifice, either of an animal, or other organic material, such as flowers, candles and incense, was seen as a means of invoking supra-human powers. The ancient word *GX*, God, is not a title, but a description, meaning "that which is invoked". Thus, by definition, a deity that cannot be invoked is not a god. In order to conduct a ceremony such as divination, the ceremonial objects must be empowered. To empower something, the empowerer infuses it with a personal aspect of the universal empowering medium, *Önd*. Every individual who has consciousness has his or her own personal power called Megin, which is named according to its qualities. The gods, for example, have *Asmegin*, and the Earth *Jardar megin* (Earth's megin), etc. Something endowed with megin becomes Magna. Thus, a stone endowed with *Megin* is *Magna steina,* a stone endowed with *megin*. Any physical object possessing *Megin* is magnat, and the modern English usage of the word *magnet* refers to a special stone or metal with the power or *Megin* to attract iron. When the magician puts *Megin* into something magically, the object becomes aukinn, augmented with the addition of the *Megin*. Thus, for example, the Norse guardian god, Heimdall, was said to be aukinn with *Jardar megin*.

When one empowers any object with Megin, it must be done in accordance with the innate nature of the materials of which the object is composed, and also the use to which it is to be put. When a spell is laid on something against its inner nature, of course, if it is done properly, then it will still work magically, but it is *älag*, an 'on-lay'. An 'on-lay' is a magical influence whose power of a different quality, yet is still dominant over the innate nature of that upon which it is laid. Divination is the reverse of the on-lay, for it intends to clarify that which is present, not to obscure it by something emanating from the will of a magician, priest or priestess. The diviner must be open to all incoming influences, which, without suitable protection, is a risky position to put oneself in. To ward off this danger, ancient Germanic and Norse diviners carried a special staff of office, recalled as an essential attribute in modern representations of wizards. Through this staff, magic was worked as well. Odin's essentially magic wand, called Gambantein, is allied to the magic staff of the seeress or sybil, Volr. Without such an empowered rod, we dare not open ourselves to the dangerous otherworldly realms without great danger.

The Cosmology of European Alphabets

Although to-day only the Roman, Greek and Cyrillic alphabets are in significant use in Europe, there were once several other serious contenders. Runes were used widely until the 1600s in Scandinavia. In 1611, there was a serious attempt by Johannes Bureus to have the runes adopted as the official alphabet of Sweden, and the printed almanacs of the 1700s continued to use them. In Estonia, runes were used on wooden calendars until the twentieth century. But, elsewhere, under different sociopolitical conditions, things were different. The runes were prohibited by the church in Iceland in 1639, and users were persecuted. The Slavonic Glagolitic alphabet went into decline around this time. But little was lost. Learned researchers, of course, knew about all the possibilities, and, on occasion, when the time was right, published valuable texts. A most remarkable example of this is the *Virga Aurea*, known in English as *The Heavenly Golden Rod of the Blessed Virgin Mary in Seventy-Two Praises*. Published by James Bonaventure Hepburn at Rome in 1616, the *Virga Aurea* contains no fewer than 72 alphabets used in Europe. Printed in the form of an engraving, this plate is a compendium of alphabets, including historical and then-current exoteric and esoteric scripts. Among the exoteric scripts are Greek, Hebrew, Roman, Hibernian, Scythian, Massagetic, Getic and Gothic, whilst among the magical ones are the Canaanite, Celestial, Supercelestial, Chaldean, Angelic and Seraphic alphabets, more the preserve of alchemists and practitioners of high magic. Of course, exoteric scripts have esoteric content, but magical alphabets are restricted to magical usage, and have rarely, if ever, been used publicly. The early 17th century was a time when a number of different alphabets could have been adopted for official use in certain countries, if events had turned out otherwise. But Europe settled for only three alphabets. This is not to suggest that a new general use of one or other of them is impossible in the future. In the West, it has happened at least twice in modern times. When political conditions were right, it was possible to restore alphabets that have passed into near-disuse. For example, the Gaelic alphabet was adopted when the Irish Free State was founded in 1921, and Hebrew became the official language of the new state of Israel in 1947.

The Gothic alphabet is one of Europe's most mysterious secrets. So much so that even its name is misused. Contrary to popular misconceptions, Gothic is not the familiar medieval *blackletter* or *fraktur* alphabet of church documents and inscriptions. This is a version of the Roman alphabet. The true Gothic is the alphabet of the Gothic nation, which, because it was used by an ethnic nation with a national church considered heretical by Catholic and Orthodox Christians, Gothic was wilfully destroyed in the year 589. However, as with everything of value, knowledge of it was preserved through the times of destruction by the innate pluralism of the world, sometimes even by those charged with its destruction. Almost one and a half thousand years later, my Gotlandia card deck of 1991, which reconstructed the meanings of the Gothic alphabet from many disparate sources, was the first Gothic divination deck ever to be published.

When they were in their ancestral homeland, which comprised northern Denmark, southern Sweden and the Baltic sacred island of Gotland, the Goths used the runes. The earliest runic inscription in Scandinavia was carved by a Goth runemaster on the famous Kylver Stone. When they adopted Arianity, Bishop Ulfila based his new alphabet upon the Gothic runes, taking also elements of Greek esoteric tradition. Along with all religions of that era, Gothic Christianity had a significant esoteric symbolic dimension. This is inherent in the structure

6. A surviving example of the Gothic alphabet in the version of the Gothic Gospels known as the Codex Argenteus. This text is a page from the Gospel According to St Mark, chapter VII.

of the Gothic alphabet. In creating the Gothic abecedary, Ulfila produced a distinct magical alphabet which was a fine medium for divination. And because of its Graeco-Scandinavian origin, Gothic has its own special character, with a unique blend of elements of the Greek and the Germanic esoteric tradition.

Like the runes, Gothic letters give us access to our place in the web of fate, the patterns of events, actions, objects, thoughts, processes and forms that make up 'now'. The Gothic letters' meanings cover every aspect of existence. When we divine with them, we see a reflection of the precise moment in time that the divination takes place. Gothic enables us to view our lives, experiences and actions in new ways. Gothic divinations are intelligible readings of the precise moment when they are made. This moment encapsulates all that has been, that is present now, and that which can follow on from it. The conditions that exist now are the result of what is called örlog in the Northern Tradition (see below). This is the combination of unchanging cosmic laws (transvolution - the way things happen) and events that have occurred in the past. The result is the present. The possibilities that we call the future are also shaped by örlog. But this is not to infer that the future is in some manner fixed or predestined. Quite the opposite. There is free-will and anything can happen within the parameters determined by örlog. We, here and now, in the present, are at the cutting-edge of reality, with the free will that consciousness brings.

Our actions are free within these constraints, but of course may and will be influenced by all manner of different considerations, seen and unseen, natural and supernatural, innate and external, conscious and unconscious. If we are to live optimally, or to understand the conditions acting upon the present, then we must strive to gain all of the available information we can about our örlog. Then we will have a more complete awareness and understanding of the state of the present, and our place within it. Divination by the Gothic staves gives us one such key to this usually-obscured area of futilely, to dispense with the past as if it had no bearing on the present, and therefore no relevance. But, as the ultimate failure of their revolutions proved, the past is vitally important, and it cannot be ignored. Its influence will be felt whether or not we want it to. This is not only because those events preceded the present as its formative causes. It is even more important that this because it constitutes an actual part of our present. That which has been is a component of that which we are, in the form of that which was. The reality of now, of our life, is of the actual present, and it cannot be removed.

Nothing exists unless it is present now in some form or other. If anything of the past exists at all, then its existence is in the form of something present within us as living beings. The past does not exist in some external, preserved, way, which can be pulled out of limbo at will as part of some intact cosmic record like a forgotten file on a computer diskette. That part of it which is here is present now. The rest is gone, and only its implicit results are present. In talking of it, in acting upon it, we are re-membering the past. As present beings, we are continuous with the past, just as we are continuous with our environment. The present exists as a continuation of its örlog. Our lives, as part of this örlog are composed of what we have been, both in the individual and collective realms. It is through divination that we can unravel for a fleeting moment the threads of this Web of Wyrd, and gain some meaningful viewpoint which otherwise we might never have had.

Cosmic Viewpoints

The remit of science as a human activity is limited to finding substantial, measurable, things that are subject to being separated from one another, divided and analysed fragment by fragment, piece by piece. Although it is patently not the case, science treats reality as if it is also a world of separate things arranged in neutral space. Even the seamless mystery of time

8. In the Pagan tradition, cosmic order is often personified by a goddess who brings order out of chaos. The Latin motto of the Honourable Guild of Locators, *Ordo ab Chao*, "From Chaos, Order", recognises the necessity for order that takes account of the flow of events. Thus, it is not inflexible, but eminently appropriate at all times.

7. In Gothic divination, we recognise that to us the Cosmic Flow is the most important aspect of our immediate existence. The traditional arts of Germanic and Celtic peoples recognise this in their interlaced and spiral knot-work.

continuum. But this is beyond the remit or capability of the scientific method. It is because it can be expressed only in a symbolic language that is present both in nature and human consciousness, that divinatory systems came into being. In their fully-developed form, the alphabets used in divination - such as the Runes, Ogham, Greek and Gothic - are genuinely neutral symbolic languages whose use can enable those that use them the means to acquire some meaningful understanding of these time-qualities, and to express them in a useful way.

In the present work, because the Gothic alphabet is derived in its structure, if not its form, from the Northern Tradition, I describe the underlying, primal influence of existence by a Norse name, örlog. Literally, the word örlog means 'primal laws', or 'underlying layers'. According to tradition, örlog was personified sometimes as the goddess whose activities and actions lie behind or underpin fate. But it is not very helpful if we view its workings literalistically as the result of an external agency in the form of a humanoid being, however powerful, for örlog is not external to existence, neither is it operated from outside. A more useful viewpoint understands örlog as a basic principle acting within the cosmos. örlog is the present effect of those events and things which have taken place or been in existence in the past. Their former existence make the present what it is today. Sometimes, örlog is interpreted as meaning fate or destiny, but these translations do not express the inner meaning of the word. Örlog does not imply predestination as the word fate or destiny may, and it should not be mistaken for concepts of predestination, which have no place in a cosmos of indeterminacy.

The nature of time is such that past things, events and acts, even when they have been utterly obliterated, are still implicit in the present. Everything that ever happened, however minute, still has had an effect upon the making of now. But, for whatever reason, some humans refuse to acknowledge this irrefutable truth. Occasionally, revolutionists have attempted, existence. Of course this world-view, like all human views of existence, is necessarily symbolic or poetic. Believing that any world-view can be taken as literally true under all conditions and at all times, is fundamentalistic and unhelpful to a balanced view of life.

Örlog

It is an inherent limitation of material existence that there is no means by which anyone can determine whether or not the physical laws that govern the universe are constant for all time. It is a possibility - distasteful or terrifying to some - that the physical laws of existence change and evolve as if the universe were an organism or a colony of organisms. But because this question is asked rarely, and there is no means of determining any answer in any case, we must utilise our present understanding of the universe, however incomplete it may be as an approximation that is more-or-less accurate for the time in which we exist. Practically, we can only use that which works, whether or not its theoretical base is known. Magic and divination are two areas of human experience where that which works may outstrip the theoretical knowledge of how or why it works. Each and every of the theories concerning magic and divination are flawed in some way or other, giving us, at best, incomplete descriptions of how they work. But, if we apply them appropriately and correctly, they do work for us, and we should not lose sight of the fact.

One of the seemingly basic principles underlying runic divination, indeed, all divination in the European tradition, is that all points in the continuum that scientists like to call space-time have an unique quality. Because of this, every event associated with any point in this space-time continuum contains, in some subtle way, the quality of that moment. This means that theoretically the unique quality of each individual point in space-time can be discovered or revealed by investigating its relationship to every other point in that can be measured, so it is claimed, by breaking it up into arbitrary countable units, each separate from but also identical with each other. By so doing, science makes a commendable attempt to describe reality and explain existence, and, within this brief, it is very successful, producing useful results.

The traditional view of the cosmos, as expressed in the perennial philosophy, however, differs radically from the fragmental-reductionist view of science. Many traditions view the Cosmos poetically in terms of a goddess who holds within her body the various perceptible aspects or levels of existence, number, space and time. She is not a creatrix, external to existence, for she is the cosmos herself, without beginning and end, bornless and eternal, self-ordering and infinitely polyvalent. In the Northern Tradition, the cosmic goddess is known as Frigg, who, as Queen of Heaven, carries the spindle of the Nowl (the Pole Star), and the distaff that is the constellation better known by its Graeco-Arabic name as the Belt of Orion. Symbolically, the entire starry heavens are the dark cloak of Frigg. In Christian mythology, she appears too. There, her attributes were assimilated into Our Lady, who is called either the Queen of Heaven or Stella Maris, the Star of the Sea. Whatever names she is known by, this goddess is the archetype of time and space. Perhaps Frigg and Our Lady, as Queen of Heaven, may be a more recent development of the archaic fate-goddess Wurt or Wyrd. She is a threefold divine being of past, present and future, personified more frequently as the three goddesses of time and process, known variously as the Moirae, Fates, Norns and Weird Sisters. Only in minimalist religions of the book, where the written word, however unbelievable, is taught to be the absolute truth, is this symbolic, metaphorical, view of the world rejected. In places where this narrow view is imposed by force, as in fundamentalist states, life and spiritual existence is impoverished thereby.

In traditional art, the cosmos is also represented sometimes as a grid. Naturally, this pre-dates by millennia the ubiquitous use of the grid in the West as the basis for scientific mathematical representation. Before the days of Descartes, however, the traditional European metaphor of the space-time flow was as the woven fabric, known in the Northern Tradition as The Web of Wyrd. The weft and warp of this web can be thought of symbolically as the structure of time-matter, which can be symbolised as the goddess herself. As time passes, the order, structure, colour, texture and form of these threads are changed. The first fate, the past, spins the thread; the second, who represents the present, weaves the threads into the Web of Wyrd, whilst the third destroys it. In this way, the three Weird Sisters express the reality of existence, that is that events have finality. The cosmos never turns back: none of her patterns are repeated in exactly the same way, and none of the patterns are permanent. The flow of reality can never be reconstructed: it is continuously changing with human consciousness. By observing these patterns we can illuminate temporarily particular aspects of the infinitely changing multiplicity of existence. These are the patterns that underlay and inform the ancient art of the Celts, Alamanni, Anglians and Goths are *par excellence* the artistic manifestation of Manred and the Web of Wyrd.

Coming into Being

The Northern European creation myth describes a natural process during which the gods, human beings, the elves, dwarfs, giants and the Earth herself come into being. This is the initial formation of the Web of Wyrd. It is this awareness of natural process that underlies the runes and Gothic alphabet. According to Norse tradition, before order emerged, there was nothing but chaos:

"In archaic ages, when roarings sounded,
There was no sand, nor sea, nor briny water,
No earth below, no heaven above,
Only the yawning deep, bearing no growth."

This yawning deep was Ginnungagap, infinite empty space. But although there was chaos, there was direction: principle of orientation existed. Within the framework of direction, along an axial line in space, symbolically the first thread of the Web of Wyrd, chaos resolved itself into a polarity of north and south. In the north was ice and in the south, fire. The north carried the static, crystalline principle of ice and darkness, whilst the south bore the active, energetic, principle of fire and light. When the two opposing principles met in the yawning deep, then, light was frozen, the chaotic particles crystallised into molecular form and matter came into existence. When we perform the traditional rite of foundation for a building, we draw on the ground the *rig*, the first line that re-enacts the process of the first coming-into-being.

The vibrational principle, described poetically by the bard as "when roarings sounded", can be seen as the energy of the cosmos. Chaos and disorder coalesced into ordered shapes that reflected in physical form the patterns of the vibrations. Order thereby emerged from chaos. Energy was all that existed to drive this newly formed matter. This roaring was personified symbolically as Ymir, the androgynous primal giant from which the matter of the world was made. In another part of the *Edda, Grimnismal*, Odin, under his by-name of Grim, tells us that:

"The flesh of Ymir made the Earth,
The sea was formed from his sweat,
Hills from his bones, high trees from his hair,
The starry sky from out of his skull."

Here, the material of the universe is viewed as having been formed from the body of sound personified in anthropomorphic form. The underlying belief expressed here is that all physical bodies, human, animal, plant or mineral, are paralleled at another level by patterns of sound. The researches of the scientists Chladni and Jenny have revealed the generation of such patterns by sound, and the techniques of sound healers are a practical application of the principles. But although cosmic and earthly matter was formed from vibration, the higher levels of order did not come into being immediately. Chladni's and Jenny's experiments with vibrating matter showed that some time is needed for stable patterns, standing waves and cellular forms, to stabilise themselves. Thus,

> "The Sun saw no seat where she should sit,
> The Moon might not mark his mightiness.
> Seemingly without standpoint were the stars;
> But Bor and his sons took up the spheres,
> And also mighty Midgard made.
> The Wise Ones went to watch and ward,
> The Holy Gods, holding high council,
> Named night and the new moon, too,
> Morning and midday moreover they named,
> Eventide too and afternoon to ordain."

The poetic view of the world expressed in this and other ancient European Pagan scripture tells us that we can understand better our place in the world when we look at it from a specific viewpoint. As humans, it is natural first to be anthropocentric in our view of existence, whilst acknowledging our awareness that this is not the only way. The Nordic text *Alvismal*, described below, shows that traditional European Paganism recognises this plurality well. The image of the primal giant Ymir is a metaphor for the elements of existence that dwell within us all, with which we can come into alignment if we try. Science, which originated in Pagan philosophy in ancient Egypt and Greece, is another means by which we can understand existence. As long as science has a spiritual, ethical element, then it is of great value. Reflecting the Hermetic maxim, "As above, so below", it can bring illumination. Together, the magical, metaphysical and the scientific viewpoints complement one another, bringing our understanding to a higher level.

Cosmic Energies

The enigmatic forces present in the earth were recognized as a reality by the people of pre-scientific, pre-industrial cultures. According to the magical-poetic world view of the Germanic skalds and the Celtic bards, these subtle forces were personified usually in the form of non-human yet sentient beings which people sometimes encountered at certain places in the landscape. Although these could appear in many different forms and under various guises, each discrete being was but a specialised manifestation of the greater whole. These manifestations are, among other things, described as fairies, gnomes, sprites, trolls, elementals, will o'the wisps and dragons. Often, places at which their qualities and virtues can be felt by people sensitive to such things, have been venerated. In the Celtic tradition, this power is described well, and is spoken of most frequently as the Nwyvre.

As a semi-abstract power, this Nwyvre is depicted commonly in the form of a mythological dragon-like beast. Although it has no biological reality, it appears throughout medieval European art. This compound reptile is shown with the head of a predatory animal, with ears. Its head is joined to a reptilian body which has one pair of legs. Its back bears wings, and its rear part is a prehensile, snake-like body and tail. The Wyvern of English heraldry, among other things, the emblem of Wessex, is depicted in the form of the classic Nwyvre. Here, it is distinguished from the very similar dragon by possessing only two legs (the dragon has four). Usually, the Wyvern's legs are forelegs, and the posterior portion of the beast is serpent-like. Images of the Nwyvre are carved in stone in many European churches, where their wings, claws and spiralling tails are prominent features that add to the interest and

9. In medieval art, the dragon or serpent is often depicted in its moment of destruction by an armour-clad knight. This is often interpreted as the suppression of European Paganism by armed force. Engraving from Olaus Magnus.

symbolic mystery of the architecture. The Nwyvre is a symbolic form that represents the elements through which this abstract force is felt. They are the classical four elements of western alchemy. The fire-breathing mouth represents fire; the legs walk upon the earth; the wings carry it through the air; and the serpentine tail denotes its ability to swim through water. In this form, the Nwyvre is universal.

According to traditions from all lands, these forces are present at sacred places. They manifest in various ways, and modern Earth Mysteries researchers have linked this legendary power of the Nwyvre with the forces generated by underground water or other physical phenomena that skilled practitioners of the divining rod profess to detect. Linguistically, the word Nwyvre is derived from the Indo-European root *wed*, which means water. The cognate Gallic word *Vobero* has the more specific meaning of underground water, which links it to the spiral pattern of subterranean streams, which water diviners understand well. In classical alchemical descriptions, this force is known as the *quintessence*, whilst in Scandinavia, the power personified in fire, air, water and earth, was known more abstractly as önd, which interpenetrates all of material existence. The Celts personified it in the human being as deo, the 'divine spark'. Whatever it is called, and however it is depicted, this force or energy can be visualized as that vital power which drives existence.

In modern Welsh, the related word *nwyf* means energy, *nwyfriant*, vigour and vivacity, whilst *nwyfre* means the sky or 'firmament'. The nature of this subtle force is described in the collection of ancient Welsh texts that explain the elements of Bardism, *Barddas*. One text included in *Barddas* describes the five elements, as: "*Calas*; fluidity; breath; uvel and nwyvre. From *calas* is every corporeity, namely, the earth and every thing hard; from *fluidity* are moisture and flux; from *breath* are every wind, breeze, respiration and air; from *uvel* are all heat; fire and light; and from *nwyvre* every life and motion, every spirit, every soul of man, and from its union with the

10. Woden, the seeker-after-wisdom who, after undertaking dangerous and life-threatening ordeals, discovered the runes and gave them to the human race.

other elements, other living beings". Some versions of the Bardic five elements text use the word *nev* instead of Nwyvre. It is likely that this word, *nef,* a word used in modern Welsh to denote heaven, is the same as the ancient Egyptian term, *neph,* the force that pervades and animates the entire world. As human beings, emanating from the earth as living manifestation of the material world, we are subject to the forces and powers that flow through all of the other elements of the world. Thus, the ancients saw in the human being a reflection of the cosmos, according to the maxim, attributed to the divine Egyptian sage, Hermes Trismegistus, "As above, so below". Thus, however it is expressed in all its pluralistic variety, the perennial philosophy sees that we human beings are not meaningless, worthless parasites upon a hostile, aimless planet, but integral parts of existence. As individual reflections of the cosmos, we are the conscious representatives of all existence, and thus we partake of divine nature.

Chapter 3
The Origin of Wisdom

We can reach a better understanding of the meanings of the Runes and the Gothic alphabet when we look at the inner meaning of certain aspects of Northern Tradition mythology from Germanic, Norse and Celtic sources. An account emerges of deliberate consciousness-alteration and the consequent realisation of new insights which transform not only the discoverer, but also, through him, wider society. According to recorded myths, legends and folk-tales, at a certain point in history, the older Germanic gods of flocks and fields, earth and water, the Vanir, were challenged by the newer, more civilised, gods of order and progress, the Aesir. Inevitably, they fought a war to decide which way the world would go, the outcome of which, as in all impossible conflicts between eternal principles, was inconclusive. When the war between the Aesir and the Vanir finally came to a stalemate, it ended in truce. The armistice was sealed by a pact in which every god and goddess made an oath which was hallowed when each spat into a vessel. From this divine spittle arose a being called Kvasir, a wise and good person who then travelled the world dispensing wisdom. Kvasir came into being at the time when the divine representatives of fecundity and prosperity, the Vanir, became allied to those of force and sovereignty, the Aesir. The name Kvasir means literally 'the juice of crushed fruits', cognate with the English word 'squash', related to the Slavonic Kvas, which is an alcoholic drink. .

According to Norse myth, when the bright solar god Balder was slain by the mistletoe branch by Loki's agency, Odin, Thor and Kvasir set out to catch the perpetrator of the heinous crime. Loki, who had set up the conditions for the killing, fled to a a house which had doors facing the four cardinal directions, so that he could see anyone coming from any direction. So, when the gods approached, he saw them coming. It gave him the chance to escape by changing himself into a salmon, in which shape he swam away down the waterfalls of the Fraananger. Loki knew that although he could evade any hook-and-line, nevertheless he could be caught by a net like that he had borrowed once from his sister, the sea-goddess Ran. He had used the net to capture a shape-shifted dwarf, Andvari. Loki therefore experimented to see how he could best escape from a similar net if the gods should decide to use one against him. Therefore he made one for himself.. But, when he saw the gods coming after him, he burnt it in the fire-place so they would not know what he had been doing. Arriving at Loki's house, Kvasir looked at the hearth, and immediately saw in the pattern of ashes the remains of the net, and realised at once that this was the only way to catch the Salmon-Loki. Then the gods made a new net to Kvasir's pattern, and, at the third try caught Loki, whom they bound to three stones using the entrails of his son, Narve. Once Loki was bound, these entrails were magically transmuted into iron fetters, and Loki was held captive there by them until Ragnarök.

Subsequently, during his later travels dispensing wisdom, Kvasir was murdered in his sleep by two treacherous dwarves, Fialar and Galar. In his martyrdom, his blood was drained into three vessels. They were a cauldron whose name was Odhroerir, and two smaller sacrificial bowls, Son and Boden, whose names mean 'expiation' and 'offering' respectively. Fialar and Galar mixed Kvasir's blood with honey, and it fermented naturally into a mead which had magical properties so that anyone who drank some would be sure to gain the power of poetry. Thus was the blood of Kvasir called "the mead of poetry and wisdom". A kenning for poetry, based on this story, was "Kvasir's Blood". Having created this magic brew, the dwarves hid the containers in a safe place and continued on their killing expedition. They encountered Gilling, a giant, whom they took out to sea in a boat and drowned. Then they killed his giantess wife by dropping a mill-stone on her head from the roof of her house. These mindless murders brought down a blood-feud upon Fialar and Galar. Suttung, Gilling's brother, went looking for them, and finally tracked down the dwarves. He took them prisoner, and carried them by ship to a sandbank in the sea that would be covered at high tide, intending to abandon them there to drown. But, to bribe Suttung into sparing them, they offered him the strange brew in exchange for their lives. He agreed, and they led him to the hiding-place. The dwarves then gave the mead to Suttung, who released them. The giant gave it into the safe keeping of Gunlod, his daughter. She retired to a cave in a hollow mountain, being told by Suttung that she should let no-one taste the mead.

But, during their flights across the world, Hugin and Munin, Odin's ravens, perceived the mead and told their master of its existence. Travelling to the locality in the guise of Bolwerk, a name meaning 'The Ill-Doer', Odin encountered nine peasants with scythes mowing a field. Producing a fine whetstone, he taunted them with it, then through it among them. The peasants fought for the whetstone, and cut one another to pieces with their scythes until all of them were killed or died of their wounds. Then Bolwerk-Odin went to their master, the giant Baugi, who was the brother of Gilling and Suttung. As his serfs were dead now, Bolwerk-Odin offered to do the nine peasants' work for a season in return for a draught of the mead of poetry and wisdom.

After finishing the work in a supernaturally short time, Odin went to Baugi for his recompense. As Gunlod had been ordered not to dispense the mead to anyone, Baugi agreed to get the mead by deception. With Bolwerk-Odin, Baugi went to the hollow mountain, but Gunlod would not let them in. Then Bolwerk-Odin produced Rati, his auger, and used it to drill through the mountain to reach the cave. He shape-shifted into a serpent which crawled through the drilled hole into Gunlod's presence. Inside the cave, Bolwerk-Odin transformed back into manly form, and made love with Gunlod for three days. Each day, Bolwerk-Odin asked for a just a sip from each vessel, but instead, each time, drank all of the mead in the container.

At the end of his three days' love-making and mead-drinking, Odin emerged from the cave, and shape-shifted into the form of an eagle. When Suttung discovered that the mead was consumed, he too changed into eagle's form and set off in pursuit of Eagle-Odin. Eagle-Odin flew back to Asgard, and landed before Suttung. He bade the Aesir to build a fire on the ramparts of Asgard. As Suttung flew over it, he was burnt and killed.

Then Odin regurgitated the mead he had drunk in the cave of Gunlod. In haste, some drops of the mead were lost. They fell to Middle Earth, where as "the poetasters' share", they continue to inspire human bards to this day. Nine months after Odin's visit, Gunlod gave birth to Bragi, god of eloquence and poetry, who emerged from the hollow mountain in a boat. Because the dwarves were forced to give up the mead on board ship, poetry was sometimes called "The Ship of the Dwarves". Traditionally, toasts to eloquence, sacred to Bragi, were drunk from a boat-shaped cup, the Bragaful. The 5000 year-old chambered cairn at Newgrange contained three boat-shaped stone basins which echo this practice and the three vessels of Kvasir's blood.

Symbolically, the hollow mountain that Odin penetrates in snake-form can be interpreted as a womb containing the archetypal menstrual blood, which the initiate drinks during ritual cunnilingus in order to gain illumination. This is one of the important keys to the ritual sexuality practised by initiates of the Nameless Art. This, and other sexual practices, like *Drewary*, were once viewed by non-practitioners as being so obscene that they were never written about, being referred to only vaguely as "unspeakable rites". Because the practice of

11. The Goddess in the Labyrinth.

sacred sexuality was the preserve of relatively few people at any one time, and all sexuality except for procreation was disapproved of by the Christian priesthood, the whole matter of illumination through sexuality has remained hidden in northern European culture. Such things are more associated in the modern mind with the *Kama Sutra* and Tantra than with indigenous European practice.

However, there are still many keys to this hidden sexual tradition. The position in which we view the carvings called Sheela-na-Gigs is the actual view of the woman that the initiate sees during the ceremony alluded to in the legend of Kvasir's blood. The woman's breasts are invisible through foreshortening, whilst the vulva and face are prominent. Her hands hold herself open so that the man is free to drink her menstrual blood. The common name for these carvings, Sheela-na-Gig is Irish, but its Scots Gaelic version, Sile-na-Gcioc, seems more significant. Literally, it means 'Julia of the Breasts', singularly inappropriate for a breastless vulva-oriented representation, and perhaps a euphemism intended to draw attention away from the obvious nature of the depictions. Yet he who drinks from both breasts as well as the vulva emulates Odin drinking from the two smaller and the one larger vessel. The name Julia is interesting on another level, for it provides us with a link to the Goddess in the Labyrinth, whose mazes, or love-nests, were often called Julian's Bower. In a few cases, the Sheela-na-Gigs are associated with carvings of erect men. A good example is the ithyphallic man who appears with the Sheela-na-Gig in a carved relief on the church at Whittlesford in Cambridgeshire. He is depicted next to the Sheela-na-Gig in a crawling position appropriate for a man about to perform cunnilingus.

According to the story, the blood of Kvasir, fermented with honey, made "the mead of poetry and wisdom". This strange brew can be seen as the Northern Tradition parallel of the ancient Indian elixir called Soma in the *Rig-Veda* and the parallel Haoma of the Zoroastrian *Avesta*. This was made by

12. Woden, as keeper of the secrets of consciousness.

pressing the material in a pestle and mortar, a technical device that may relate the Asiatic tales to the millstone used to kill the giantess. Like the blood of Kvasir, Soma or Haoma brought numinous knowledge to the initiates who partook of them. In European tradition, these drinks are identical with the Irish drink called Meath that brings the sacred gift of possession through magical intoxication. It also parallels one of the aspects of the British figure of the miracle of bread and ale, John Barleycorn, who dies so that his body can be made into food and drink for the enjoyment and sustenance of humankind. When they invented the Eucharist, Christian priests emulated these older traditions in the ceremony of bread and wine.

According to Northern Tradition writings, Odin's wisdom comes from two fluid sources: the blood of Kvasir and the waters guarded by Mimir. Mimir is the guardian of the holy spring at the root of Yggdrassil (whose by-names include Hoddmimir 'the Treasure of Mimir', and Mimameiⵝr, 'the Pole of Mimir') in the realm of the frost-giants. It is from this source, the Headwater of Memory, that Odin also drinks to gain enlightenment. It appears that these deities of wisdom must die and be dismembered for their powers to be disseminated. In Norse legend, Kvasir and Mimir, and in British mythology, the divine king, Bendigaidvran (Bran the Blessed), are all killed, but their powers outlive them. Mimir is said to have been a member of the Aesir, given to the Vanir as a hostage and subsequently slain by them. After he died, like Bendigaidvran, Mimir was beheaded. His head was sent to Odin, who consulted it in times of trouble. This is a direct parallel of the miraculous Bendigaidvran, whose disembodied head was carried around Britain as an oracle before being buried in the White Mount, the holy hill of London, where the White Tower of the Tower of London now stands. White hills or mountains in general (such as Mont Blanc) are the Caer Sidi or 'glass castle' of Celtic tradition (such as the quartz-clad Newgrange), in which the Cauldron of Inspiration was to be found.

The speech that emanated from Bendigaidvran's severed head allowed those who heard it to understand the song of birds, and ravens, his sacred birds, are kept at the Tower of London still. They are direct parallels of the ravens of Odin, Hugin and Munin, 'thought' and memory', and the birds that once adorned the pillars around the mausoleum of Theodoric. Perhaps Hugin and Munin originally belonged to Mimir, and not Odin. Also the *xoana,* the Gothic sacred images that were in the form a head carved at the top of a post, closely resembles the use of real human heads in this way. In Norse tradition, Mimir's head was set up over the holy spring, where it answers Odin's incantations. Until the nineteenth century, the cult of the head of inspiration continued at certain holy wells in Wales which retained the custom of drinking from a 'cauldron' made from a 'saint's' skull in order to gain knowledge, or a cure of illness. Skull-magic was very much a part of Catholic Christian practice. All over western Europe are shrines of skulls which were resorted to for healing and other magical uses. In England, Wells Cathedral, York Minster and Bury St Edmund's Abbey were three important shrines where exceptional skulls were kept, whilst to-day, skulls with jewelled eye sockets look out from the baroque the high altar of the cathedral at Konstanz in Germany.

Bendigaidvran was one of the possessors of the Celtic Cauldron of abundance. At one time, it was transported from Ireland to Britain, then returned again to the emerald isle as part of Branwen's dowry. According to Taliesin Ben Beirdd, it was brought from the underworld, Annwn, by King Arthur, who here was seen as an earthly aspect of the Celtic Ash-god of wisdom, Gwydion ap Don. The cauldron was kept in Caer Pedryvan, the four-square castle of Pwyll in the Isle of the Active Door. This four-sided castle recalls the four-doored house of Loki in the Norse legend. The Cauldron of Abundance stands over a fire that is fanned by nine maidens so that from it come oracular pronouncements. The nine orgiastic priestesses of the Breton holy island of Sein, near Carnac, who taught sexual secrets to their initiates, and the vestal keepers of the sacred flame of Brigid at Kildare are reflections of this. The Cauldron of Pwll has properties identical to those associated with that owned by the Irish god known as The Dagda, and the British cauldrons of Cerridwen and Branwen. It has the triadic powers of inexhaustibility, inspiration and regeneration. Like Odhroerir, Ceridwen's Cauldron had the property that anyone who drank from it gained the gift of divine inspiration.

One legend of the cauldron of Ceridwen has parallels with the story of the birth of Bragi. The story is located on the island in the middle of Lake Tegid in Wales. Ceridwen has a hideously ugly son, Avagddu. So that his ugliness can be compensated by wisdom, Ceridwen brews a potion of inspiration that must be boiled for a year, producing three drops of divine fluid (parallelling the three vessels of Kvasir's blood-mead). She orders her servant, Gwion, to watch over the cauldron. But accidentally, he gets the three drops on his finger, which, as in the similar story of the enlightenment of Fionn MacCumhaill, he cools by putting in his mouth. Immediately, Gwion is illuminated. Ceridwen, furious that the potion has gone to the wrong person, pursues Gwion. But, like Odin, Loki and Baugi, he is able to, shape-shift. First, he becomes a hare, then a fish, a bird, and finally a grain of winnowed wheat on the threshing-floor of a barn. Ceridwen in turn becomes a greyhound to catch the hare, an otter to catch the fish, a hawk to catch the bird, and finally a black hen.

In this form, she eats the grain of wheat, but becomes pregnant. She bears Gwion as a baby, whom she abandons, however, in a coracle at sea. Gwion, like Bragi, thereby floats away from his mother. The coracle is caught on top of a pole in the fish-weir of Gwyddno Garanhir, and the baby is rescued by Gwyddno's son, Elphin. Like Bragi, Gwion can speak in infancy. He tells Gwyddno that he is Taliesin, a 'general primary bard', who has been present in all ages. He grows up to become the greatest Bard of Britain. The lord of the region, Gwyddno Garanhir is a crane-being, whose epithet is "The

Long-Legged Stalker". Gwyddno caught fish in a traditional tidal fish-weir woven from hazel wands, parallelling the net of Ran. Also, Kvasir's entrapment of Loki in Salmon form echoes the story of Finn MacCumhaill catching Fintan, the Salmon of Wisdom, at Connla's Well, over which grew the Hazel-trees of Knowledge. Gwion, too, fled in fish-form from Ceridwen.

It appears that in the Celtic and Germanic spiritual traditions, the fundamental gender of cauldron- and spring-keepers is female. Mimir's alleged maleness appears to come from a linguistic confusion. Because in the Northern Tradition, guardians of holy wells were usually female, it is not unreasonable to suggest that Mimir was originally a giantess, just as Gunlod was guardian of the mead of Kvasir's blood, and Cerridwen guardian of the cauldron of wisdom. Throughout Northern Tradition scripture, when Odin needs magical advice, he consults wise women or goddesses. He learns Sei𝗫r from Freya, travels disguised on the advice of Frigg, consults the Norns, and rides into the underworld to consult the spirit of a dead Völva.

The holy spring of Forseti the Lawgiver, on the holy island of Heligoland, gave waters considered so sacred that any who drank of them was thereby sanctified. Cattle which had drunk Forseti's water were sacred and could not be slaughtered. At the solemn judicial assemblies held on the island, the participants drew water from the source, and drank it in silence so they could gain wisdom and insight before carrying out their functions. In the continental Germanic tradition, arbitration and law-speaking, the attributes of Forseti, were customarily done by women.

When Mimir was guardian of the source, Odin was permitted to drink only after sacrificing one of his eyes. The waters contained wisdom and understanding that requires a serious sacrifice to obtain. When he tore out an eye, Odin broke off a branch of Yggdrassil that hung over the holy well. From this ash-stave, he fashioned his magic spear, Gungnir. Thus, the moment of inspiration was marked and symbolised by wood-taking. Physiologically, the loss of an eye brings certain unavoidable alterations in the consciousness of a human being. These effects are be reproduced in a less drastic manner by practitioners of Northern Tradition posture-magic, who take up a certain stance on one leg with one eye closed. This posture is called "The Crane-Stance of Clarity". Incidentally, both in the Celtic and the Greek traditions, cranes are associated with the invention or discovery of letters, as is Odin in the Nordic.

In the Celto-Norse tradition of the Isle of Man, Manannan MacLir's sacred island, cranes served as the guardians of the door to the other worlds. Three cranes protected the entrance to the castle of the lord of the lower world, Mider. Their duty was to ward off strangers by calling to passers-by. The first would say, "Do not enter!"; the second, "Keep away!", and the third, "Pass by!". Only those who could pass the ordeal of the three cranes could enter the underworld and gain its wisdom. Representations of these three cranes are known from several Gaulish Pagan altars. There, they are usually associated with a willow tree, a bull, and sometimes the axe-god Esus. A typical example of this is the Romano-Celtic altar stone found at Treves that shows Esus with his axe standing at the foot of a tree in which are three cranes and a bull's head. Another Pagan altar was found in the foundations of the cathedral of Notre Dame at Paris, which was built upon a venerable Druidic shrine. This altar depicts three cranes standing on the back of a bull. Here, too, the Cosmic Axis appears as a willow tree.

Taliesin himself describes the Cauldron of Ceridwen as the "Sweet cauldron of the five trees", referring to the origin of the Celtic Ogham tree alphabet, inspirer of *cerddau,* poems. Just as Odin took over Mimir's wisdom, so Gwydion took over Bendigaidvran's. Befitting of their otherworldly origins, Gwydion's Ogham staves were kept and carried in a Crane-skin Bag. According to tradition, in ancient times the Celtic diviners kept their lot-twigs in a special medicine bag made from the skin of a crane. This was the Bhuilg Chraobhaich, 'The Bag of Branching Patterns', an important component of the paraphernalia of Druids, Bards and Vates. Manannan Mac Lir, Celtic god of the sea, possessed a crane-skin bag, known poetically as the Crane-Skin of Secrets, in which the wisdom of the Oghams is contained. (For further details of this, see Nigel Pennick and Nigel Jackson's forthcoming: *Celtic Mysteries*, Capall Bann,).

Manannan's bag was actually made from the skin of Aoife who had been killed in her shape-shifted state as a crane. This sacred feathered womb-like medicine-bag was "a treasure of powers with many virtues". From Manannan MacLir, the magical crane-bag passed into the guardianship of Lugh, the God of Light, and from him to the three sons of Cearmaid Honeymouth before Manannan regained it. Eventually, it came into the possession of Conaire as he slept on the hillside of Tara. This is another connection of consciousness/wisdom with the geomantic *omphalos*, for Tara is the central Navel of Ireland whose axial point is the *Lia Fail,* the Stone of Destiny. Ancient stories about magical bags of divinatory tools attest to the importance of such things to the indigenous peoples of ancient Europe. The runes and Gothic divination fall into the same category. It is likely that the Herulians carried their runes and divinatory paraphernalia in similar special bags. Perhaps something like them have been found by archaeologists, but have yet to be recognized for what they are.

During his self-sacrifice, Odin spends nine days and nine nights of ecstatic agony, suspended from the cosmic axial tree over the spring-pool below. This is a prime example of the *Khosma Principle* of Gothic spirituality, which is characterised as illumination through agony. As he is pierced with the Ash-tree spear Gungnir, created at his first eye-losing illumination, Odin's lifeblood falls into the genital fountain of Mother Earth. In the spring-pool is a horn, symbolising Odin's sacrificed eye, the reflected moon. It is also the Gjallarhorn of Heimdall. The spring-pool becomes a uterus for Odin's semen, bringing about

13. Irminsul, the column of the heavens.

his own rebirth. The horn also preserves some of the semen for later use in the cyclic regeneration of the world. Horn-blowing Heimdall has the by-name, Rigr, which may refer to his erection. (In Norse tradition, Rigr is the progenitor of the three ranks of society). At this source, one-eyed Odin, having already given up the eye connected to the analytical side of the brain, receives the intellectual means of transmitting knowledge, doing word-magic and formalized divination, the runes. In this way, he regains his analytical view through artificial means.

The connection of seership with a sacred spring is also apparent with the Norns. Their home is at the Urdar Fountain, said to be one of three springs corresponding with the three roots of Yggdrassil. The Norns' spring is located in the realm of the Aesir. Urdarbrunnen contains two swans. The magic fluid called Aurr that flows from this source is used by the Norns to water the World Tree, Yggdrassil. The remainder falls to earth as the morning dew. There, at the holy well amid the roots, the Norns, daughters of Wyrd, goddess of transvolution (the way things happen), weave the Web of Wyrd. Urd, the past, spins the thread; Verdandi, the present, weaves it into ever-evolving patterns; and Skuld, 'that which is to become', tears it apart. They work as if in trance, under the power of örlog. The Web of Wyrd stretches across the whole world from east to west, and from north to south. Everything in existence is subject to it. There is no way out, for an individual's fate is reflected in the colours of the Web of Wyrd. A death is notified by a black thread running north-south. When the Norns visit Middle Earth, they do so in the guise of swans. The net used by Kvasir to catch Loki is an example of the inexorable Web of Wyrd, parallel with the net of the sea-goddess Ran, which none can escape.

The Scottish tradition of tartan patterns denoting one's ancestry is an example of the Web of Wyrd in physical form. It is a tradition of considerable antiquity. The oldest tartan so far found dates from the third century of the Common Era. It was discovered at Falkirk in Scotland. In former times, each tartan pattern was recorded on a special Sett Stick, which, for each family, village or clan, were kept by the women who were carriers of the tradition. In his description of the Western Isles of Scotland, published in 1703, Martin Martin tells that the women there took great care to keep the exact pattern of their tartans by means of a 'piece of wood' that had 'the number of every thread of the stripe on it'. These sett sticks were slivers of wood upon which the coloured threads of the tartan were wound. James Logan, writing in *The Scottish Gael* in 1831, stated that the weavers recorded the precise instructions for the pattern "by means of a small stick, round which the exact number of threads in every bar were shown, a practice in use to this very day". The whole pattern was thus encoded very simply, being readily available for use by those who knew the secret, that is, were initiated practitioners of the craft of weaving.

The goddess who in the Northern Tradition is the Queen of Heaven, is the guardianess of this mystery. The Norse goddess Frigg, consort of Odin, carries the distaff as emblem this. In Celtic tradition, the parallel Queen of Heaven is Arianrhod, whose symbol is the wheel, also used in spinning. She is consort of Gwydion, the Celtic equivalent of Odin. Her name Ar-ri-an, the 'high fruitful mother', is connected with the Hellenic Ariadne, holder of the ball of thread that gives the clue to the labyrinth. In Northern Tradition astronomy, the Nowl (Pole Star) is Frigg's spindle, and the three stars known now as the Belt of Orion, her distaff. Later, with newer technology ousting the ancient distaff, the constellation became known as Frigg's Spinning Wheel. Giver of flax to humans, Frigg's spinning relates her to Urd. Frigg's emblem of the golden thread of life is the complementary opposite of the black thread of death sometimes woven by the Norns. Spinning yarn from a distaff is traditionally a women's art. The English word for an older unmarried virgin, is spinster.

In ancient Ireland, the women known as Banfathi would foretell events by looking at the swirling patterns in springs

14. Frigg, Queen of Heaven, riding her distaff. Image after the medieval wall-painting at Schleswig Cathedral, north Germany.

and rivers. The Old Norse name for a seeress was Völva. A Völva was primarily a diviner, parallel with the Banfathi of Ireland. Among the techniques they employed was to look at the upwelling waters of holy wells. They also used more definitive techniques, such as the runes. Both of these are methods by means of which the seeresses could look more deeply into the patterns of the Web of Wyrd, seeing through the outer shell of reality and inward to the more profound levels of existence.

Freyja is the goddess most closely associated with SeiXr, the consciousness-magic of the Northern Tradition which in former times was largely the preserve of women. The word SeiXr, not unexpectedly, has connotations of seething or boiling. This refers to the foreseer's capability of coming into conformity with the swirling patterns of being, the flow of events in the cosmos, the fundamental patterns of physical existence. These patterns are symbolised in Norse mythology as Hvergelmir, the primal seething cauldron of the creation-myth. The technique of SeiXr connects the diviner with this primal churning of matter and also to the divinatory possibilities inherent in the swirling patterns visible in natural springs of hot and cold water. Traditionally, these are sacred places of the healing goddess, such as at Bath in England, holy site of the Celtic goddess of healing and renewal, Sul, Romanised as Sulis Minerva. The name of the Irish goddess Badb means 'boiling'. She is one of the triadic goddesses of fate, Ana, Badb and Macha.

In Norse tradition, women practitioners of Seiör were called SeiXkonr. The Old English equivalent of this is Haegtessa, from which the word 'Hag' comes. The Dutch word for the wise women, Hagedisse, gave its name to the capital city of the Netherlands, Den Haag, which records the historic role as a centre of women's magic. The name Hagedis in Dutch means a lizard, the earthly representative of the Nwyvre. Sometimes whilst sitting on her platform at public ceremonies, the SeiXkonr was accompanied by assistants, who sang and

15. Freya, goddess of the wilder side of life, riding her Siberian Tiger.
Image after a wall-painting at Schleswig Cathedral, north Germany.

played music. The ceremony culminated with questions being answered in oracular fashion. If a man practised Seiör, it was necessary to dress as a female. This shamanic transvestism is known from both Central Asia and North America. According to Northern Tradition scripture, when Odin needed magical advice, he consulted goddesses. He learns Seiör from Freya. But it is Odin who brings the runes out of the realm of mystery for the use of all. Alluding to his access to female magic, some of Odin's by-names infer the sexual ambiguity of the shaman. Both Völvas and Seiᛉkonr would travel round the countryside, receiving hospitality and being fêted at feasts and ceremonies where they would foretell events and solve people's problems. "Wise women used to go about the land. They were called Spae-Wives and they told people's fortunes. Because of this, people would invite them into their homes and give them hospitality, and present them with gifts when they left", the Icelandic *Flateyjarbók* tells us.

In all of the wisdom-legends, the geomantic motif of the cosmic axis is present to a greater or lesser extent. The motif of the World Axis Tree with the waters of the underworld at its feet is very significant. Whilst the source of wisdom is in the waters, its transmission is through wood. When Odin gives up his eye, he takes a branch of the tree, which becomes his spear or runestaff. In ancient Celtic literature, the word 'tree' generally denotes a letter of the magical alphabet.

A basic assumption of this tradition is that knowledge is related to trees and written on wood, usually, but not always, by men, and the Gothic letter Manna has just that meaning. This ancient European wood-wisdom remains especially strong in the Welsh language, where the word *wydd* - wood is an element in words which relate to knowledge or literature. Thus, in modern Welsh, *Arwydd* is a sign, and *egwyddawr,* an alphabet. *Cyfarwydd* means skilful, that is, someone with the knowledge and ability of how to do things, whilst cyfarwyddyd is information. *Cywydd* is a revelation, whilst *dedwydd* means " having received knowledge". From this also come the words *derwydd* a druid, and *gwyddon,* a wise man, hence Gwydion. Finally, *Gwynwyddigion* are the men of sacred knowledge.

Like Odin, the Celtic god Gwydion is the shamanic god of wisdom who visits the underworld, and is associated in general with cunning and secret lore. Also like Woden, his name is revealing, for it is part of the *wydd* complex. *Gwydd* also means goose, the bird-totem of dark underworld knowledge, and the provider of the quills with which knowledge was written on parchment. Gwydion's name is another manifestation of the Indo-European root word *vid,* meaning "wise". The name Woden, as the one who has the frenzy of enlightenment, is related directly to these Celtic words, emphasising the common origin in ancient central Europe of the Celtic and Teutonic branches of the Northern Tradition. Woden and Gwydion are clearly the same archetype. Both are perfect examples of *gwynwyddigion,* who can view the world from many directions and integrate what he or she sees into a holistic vision of reality.

The Pluralistic Pagan Viewpoint

Through these techniques of consciousness, which are quite alien to all modern systems of education, the Pagans of ancient Europe had an inner understanding of pluralism. In the formative age of these techniques, the Celtic and Germanic tribes lived in societies that were in constant contact with peoples with other ways and other beliefs. Their beliefs and traditions were conducted and transmitted orally, for they had no written texts that could fix and fossilise belief, doctrine and practice. Each event conducted by each practitioner was thus a unique, present event.

Everything in existence can be viewed from several different viewpoints. No one is more correct than any other, nor more incorrect, it is just that the viewer has his or her own interpretation, so long as the reality of the thing in question is not denied. Only by understanding and comparing all viewpoints can we come to the most complete understanding possible. This pluralistic, Pagan truth is expressed in symbolic, poetic terms in *Alvismal (The Lay of Alvis)* in the *Edda*. It tells the story of Alvis, a dwarf who went to the home of the gods, Asgard, to take as his bride, Thrud, who ewas one of the daughters of the god Thor. Knowing that dwarves were wise and enjoyed displaying their learning, Thor asked Alvis, whose name means the All-Wise, to describe the thirteen most significant things in the world, according to the four viewpoints of humans, gods, giants and the dwarfish-elven folk. For the Earth, for example, Alvis told Thor, humans say earth. The gods refer to earth as fields and ways; the giants as the evergreen place; whilst the elves and dwarves call it clay, or the growing place. As there are 52 descriptions, the following table best demonstrates the different viewpoints of men and women; gods and goddesses; giants and giantesses; elvish and dwarven folk.

	Humans	Gods	Giants	Dwarves
1. Earth	earth	fields and ways	evergreen place	clay, growing place
2. Heaven	heaven	warmer of the heights	the wind weaver	high home, fair roof
3. Moon	moon	mock sun	night traveller	month-shower, whirling wheel
4. Sun	sun, Sol	shining orb	ever bright	fair wheel, Dvalin's delight
5. Wind	wind	noise-maker	wailer	roaring traveller
6. Calm	calm	quietness	wind's husk	day's refuge
7. Clouds	sky	shower bringers	wind-floes	rain-bearers, helmets of darkness
8. Ocean	sea	home of waves	home of eels	the big drink, the deep
9. Fire	fire	flamer	greedy one	burner, furnace, destroyer
10. Wood	wood	shelter of the fields	fuel	adorner of the hills, fair limbs

16. The four elements in the European tradition are symbolised by various forms of the triangle. They are air, fire, earth and water, each of which is regent of certain aspects of human life.

11. Seed	barley	grain, grower	food maker	maker of slender stalks
12. Ale	beer	foamer	swill	good cheer, mead
13. Night	night	darkness	day's mask	unlight, bringer of dreams.

Alvismal is important because it describes four different world-views. This is a classical way of looking at the world, best known in the traditional four elements of European spirituality, and the four suits of the Tarot deck. All four views in *Alvismal* are presented as being equally valid, reflecting the pluralistic understanding of the things that characterise European Pagan philosophy. Human beings describe existence with words for things; the gods see things in terms of their function or mode of doing; the giants see the world in practical, materialistic terms; whilst the dwarves and elves describe the world in metaphorical, poetic, terms. The fourfold form of Alvis's description of the world is related numerologically to the four seasons and the 52 weeks of the year. It is the format adopted by the makers of the traditional European playing-card deck, with four suits each of 13 cards. The author is working at present on a divination card deck which expresses the 52 aspects of existence in *Alvismal.*

The Craft of the Wise Women

Although men have written down their words, and oratory and poetry has long been the preserve of male practitioners, it is women who have always been the primary carriers of language and oral communication. Almost everyone learned to speak 'at mother's knee', common knowledge to the point where this truism is almost a cliché.

Women have also been the primal guardians of human iconography, possessing and transmitting the knowledge of symbols in the 'rune hoard', that preceded and defined the

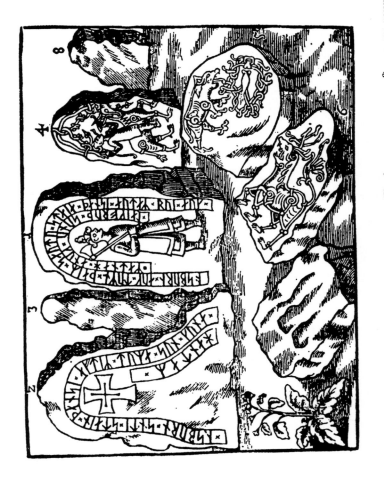

17. Scandinavian runestones, as seen by a renaissance artist. The later runes were often more rounded than their earlier counterparts, inscribed within serpent- or dragon-ribbons that often seem to represent the Nwyvre. Such stones were erected as memorials and/or magical protection.

meanings of the runes. These signs, sigils and symbols were present in the most archaic European cultures, later manifested in the various currents of indigenous European civilization.

Our oldest written records of these alphabetical meanings comes from the three Rune Poems - Anglo-Saxon, Norwegian and Icelandic - and some other poetic material. But it is certain that the meanings of some of the runes pre-dates their use as an alphabet. With others, it is less likely. Effectively, however, the detailed meanings that we have all come from the heroic tradition, a time with which the runes are most usually associated to-day. This was a patriarchal, male-dominated age of warriors and Vikings, battle-heroism and braggadocio. In more recent times, with industrialisation, their chronomantic, handicraft and agricultural uses have fallen into obscurity, whilst their association with the warrior-cult has been overemphasised. Because of this, sometimes the runes themselves have been criticised as having little to do with women's interests and pursuits, for these historic descriptions appear to make no mention of certain aspects of existence, such as, for example, the moon. However, the complementary text, *Alvismal*, which is not runic, is in some ways more balanced and complete.

Also, because the common way of writing runes was on to hard materials using a sharp object or scribing tool, they are usually angular letters, and therefore generally considered male in aspect. This, too is no more than a convention, which is no way an integral necessity for the Germanic magical alphabets. The Gothic forms, for instance, are mostly cursive. Also, historically, from the late medieval period, curving runic forms were used in Scandinavia, especially in Sweden. Inscriptions there were made by stone-masons, and runic type-faces, influenced by Venetian models, were employed by printers. When we work with the curving forms of runes, we can perceive quite different aspects of their existence. The Gothic letters are particularly useful in this respect. Also, the meanings of the runes given in the Rune Poems are only outward expressions: an animal or object actually represents an inner essence, transcendent nature or archetype. These inner meanings of the Germanic alphabets apply equally to male and female, for they are transcendent of gender.

Symbolically, there are two basic principles of handwork, which can be associated with the two genders. The male force can be exemplified by the use of direct fire in processing the inanimate. It uses hot materials, and compels them by reciprocal, hammering motion, forcing them into shape by moulds and stamps, fixing them with rivets and nails. The imposition of mechanic form upon the material world, and entering the surface of the earth by ploughing, are both techniques traditionally associated with male ways of doing things. The female ways use indirect fire. They process the animate, using rotation, continuous, spinning, weaving and knotting. The female way creates organic form by building up gradually, sowing, tending, growing and harvesting. In the Northern Tradition, these aspects are personified by two deities, Thor and Frigg. Thor is the epitome of male power, the Hammerman who uses his physical strength to alter and create. Frigg, the goddess with the distaff, is the spinster, but without the pejorative connotations of the word. She is the personification and conductress of the handicrafts traditionally associated in Europe with women: carpets, clothing, painted 'folk art', 'ornament', ceramics, pottery, glass beadwork, all of which contain the inner knowledge of craft.

With the advent of the factory world, and the concomitant commercialisation and male dominance of professions, women gradually lost control of their traditional trades. With this loss of control came a dwindling of the knowledge of their inner lore. Traditional body knowledge, too, was overridden by male academic theoretical medicine. Midwifery, formerly the preserve of the handywoman, was taken over or directed by male doctors. Male medicine ignored traditional women's techniques, including magical ones like the loosing-runes used in childbirth, and the herbs used to procure abortion. The handywomen's herbal lore of medicine was replaced by industrial pharmacy.

The arts of the weaving sisters were also driven down by the factory world. Weaving was mechanised, and the fabric's colours and then the materials themselves, came no longer from the natural world, with all of the spiritual correspondences inherent in plants and minerals, but from chemistry. Men began to design fashionable patterns that superseded traditional ones. The symbolic meanings were discounted by the world of fashion, which was interested in the main only with appearance and profit.Thus the women's knowledge of symbolic fabric patterns, their techniques of dyeing, and the herbal lore of colour dwindled. Later, knitting, too, was mechanised, and published patterns marketed to replace the traditional ones used at home. Traditional craft, however, is contemplation: the Goddess is beautiful, and She loves beauty. Of course, this is not the ethos of the factory, for it is the antithesis of consumerism and the reign of quantity. However, as in the past, the runes have accommodated themselves to the prevailing culture of this era, and, if the female side of the Germanic alphabets are to be restored, then likewise it must be nurtured and presented in a form which enables it to survive and flourish under present conditions.

North Italic

18. The North Italic alphabet, derived from that of the Etruscans, is said by many to be a forerunner of the runes.

Part II: The Meanings and Correspondences of the Gothic Runes and Staves

Chapter 4
Records of Northern Tradition Letter-Systems

Northern Tradition letter-systems are based upon the principle of correspondences, which give them a considerable value in divination. Firstly, each rune and letter of the alphabet signifies a phonetic value, which can be used in writing, calls and chants. Each character also possesses its own name, which expresses a meaning that itself is the starting-point for a whole system of corresponding concepts. The character's name, such as Ice for the rune Eis, contains a wealth of corresponding meanings in both the physical and psychic realms. The meanings given here are for the 24-rune Elder Futhark. They are the author's interpretations, derived from meanings in the three rune-poems, the *Vienna Codex*, the *Abecedarium Nordmannicum* and other significant texts, viewed from a goddess-orientation. The corresponding dates are from the Runic time-cycles taught by The Way of the Eight Winds. These correspondences are given as a guide to the reader for contemplation, experiment and further work.

Naturally, as nothing is eternally fixed, all of the characters' meanings are open to further interpretation on both the intellectual and intuitive levels. The whole Gothic system must be understood as being a symbolic representation of the world, for which a literalistic approach is inappropriate. We must remember that "in literalism lies madness", as the insightful psychiatrist Alfred Adler warned. When we use the symbolic approach, we can grasp and understand many truths that are elusive to literalistic and fundamentalistic approaches. It is through the symbolic realm that the Bardic way proceeds, of which the Runes and Gothic alphabets, along with the Celtic Oghams, are a significant part.

The earliest recognizable runic alphabet (more properly *futhark*, after the letter order F - U - Th - A - R - K) is known as the Elder Futhark. Like the Greek alphabet, it is composed of 24 characters. In the Elder Futhark, there are three divisions, called Aettir. Each contains eight runes. The letters of the Gothic alphabet are arranged in the same way for convenience, with the final letter, Quertra, as the last. The oldest complete rune-row in existence was carved by a Gothic rune-master or rune-mistress. In his *Runorna i Sverige*, published at Uppsala in 1928, Otto von Friesen reconstructed what he considered to be the early Gothic forms of the runes, including their genders. They are as follows:

faihu	M	cattle, property
urus	M	aurochs
thauris	M	giant/troll
ansus	M	a god
raida	F	chariot
kusma	M	abscess
giba	F	gift
winja	F	pasture
hagl	N	hailstone
nauths	F	need
eis	N	ice
jer	N	year
aihs	M	yew/bow
pairthra	F	meaning uncertain
algs	M	elk
sauil	N	sun
Tiews	M	the god Tiewaz
bairkan	F	birch/ birch rod
egeis	M	horse
manna	M	man
lagus	M	water
Iggws	M	the god Yngvi/Ing
othal	N	patrimony, inherited land
dags	M	day

(F = feminine; M = masculine; N = neuter.)

19. The Gothic runes and the staves of the Gothic alphabet.

Chapter 5
Runic and Gothic Characters' Meanings and Exegesis

The characters of Ulfila's Gothic alphabet are based directly upon the earlier runes used by the Goths. They contain implicitly all of the runes' meanings, to which are added further insights derived from Greek Pagan mysticism and Gnostic parallels. The Gothic runes and characters are as follows:

The First Aett

1. Faihu,(F). Well-being, fecundity, prosperity.
(June 29 - July 3)

The first rune is Faihu, whose sound is 'F'. It represents beginning, referring more specifically to the primal cow of Northern Tradition mythology, Audhumla, whose name means 'The Nourisher'. The Norse creation myth tells how the primal cow, Audhumla, licks salt from a crystalline block of ice. Then Buri, whose name means 'The Producer', the primal ancestor of the goddesses and gods, emerges gradually from the ice as she licks it away. In this way, Faihu symbolises the power that facilitates, denoting the common origin-point of us all. In European Pagan tradition, the white, horned, milk-giving moon-cow is a manifestation of the Great Mother in her aspect of preserver and nurturer. From her udder flow four milky streams, nourishing the Earth and all of her inhabitants. She is the creatrix and sustainer of wealth for all, not in the sense of individual possessions, but as plenty.

More developed, materialistic, ideas of wealth saw the cow as a human possession, giving Faihu its more common meaning as negotiable wealth, measured in head of cattle; in current contemporary terms, this is money. But as a principle, the rune Faihu denotes the power to attain material success, and retain it. Because of this, Faihu is used for power and personal control in any situation. It gives us all of the energy we need.

The corresponding Gothic letter, Fe, also means cattle, the traditional measure of mobile wealth, negotiable property. As a Gothic letter, the rune is extended to represent the accumulation of power, and given a more masculine interpretation as the male generative symbol, the phallus. Its parallel meaning is abundance, the gift of the Classical goddess Abundantia. As goddess of fecundity, Abundantia is comparable with the Northern Vanic goddess, Freyja, who rules the rune along with the generative, phallic god, Frey.

The Asyn Freyja is one of the ancient goddesses of northern Europe. She is a Vanic goddess stemming from pre-agricultural times, representing the qualities and values of the ancient society of hunters. She is also the goddess of love, free sexuality, fertility, shamanic magic and hunting. Her name means The Lady, corresponding with her consort-brother Frey, The Lord. Freyja's attributes can be contrasted with those of the goddess Frigg, who is the goddess of agricultural civilization, the traditional married life of the woman in a settled, state. Freyja is depicted sometimes in a chariot or cart pulled by cats. Also she is shown riding a cat or tiger. Conversely, Frigg rides a distaff, symbol of the woman's craft of spinning thread.

In south-eastern Europe, the goddess riding a great cat is the Great Goddess Cybele, often depicted mounted on a lion or tiger, or sometimes with dragons or in a chariot drawn by lions. However depicted, she was venerated in central Europe as well as in the south, and one of her cult-objects, the Gundestrup Cauldron, of partly Celtic and partly Slavic reduced to a picture, existing only through representation, the creature of the human's creation, is not reality, but a pale and distorted reflection of it.

2. Urus (U), Primal Strength
(July 14 - July 28).

Urus is the rune of Urd, the first, primal, norn, 'That Which Was', who denotes the basic grounding of that which is now. She is an aspect of the primal goddess of active existence, who has many names including Urda, Urtha, Eartha, Wurt and Wyrd. In Christian tradition, she is Eve, ancestral mother of humankind, and Anna, mother of Our Lady, an ancestral grandmother figure, who, as tutelary deity of holy wells and springs, nurtures the basic necessity of human life. Thus, the rune Urus signifies awesome strength which cannot be defeated. The rune gives direct communion with the primal, boundless power of the universe, giving us strength, stamina and perseverance. It provides a basic empowerment for anything which requires a solid grounding. But it can never be used selfishly, owned or controlled by a single individual. The power of Urus will be effective only "for the good of all".

Symbolically, the rune represents the Aurochs, the primal wild cattle of ancient Europe, (*Bos primigenus*), sadly, extinct, since the last individual was shot in Poland in 1627. In former times, the Aurochs was among the most powerful wild animals in Europe. Only the Bison and Elk were equal in strength. Unlike domestic cattle, the Aurochs was wild and tameless. The most notable features of the Aurochs were its long, sharp, curving horns. Because of their exceptional length and capacity, they were seen as symbols of the Horn of Plenty of the Goddess. People who drank from an Aurochs horn were assured of good fortune and abundance. As drinking horns, they represent the sacred spring of the Goddess, Urdabrunnr, giver of life and awareness. Their white colour reflects the white thread of Urd. The classical goddess Europa, whose

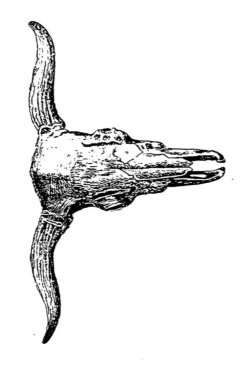

20. A skull of an Aurochs, the extinct native cattle of Europe, exterminated between 1200 and 1627. This is the symbol of the character Uras - Uraz.

workmanship, still exists. Like the continental Celts, the later Goths were at the meeting-point of northern and southern traditions in Europe, and their pantheon contained elements from both. These complex connections emphasise the difficulty we face when we attempt to draw hard-and-fast distinctions between the deities of northern and southern Europe, Celtic, Germanic, Greek and Anatolian, for all are multivalent aspects of the archetypal gods and goddesses which manifest daily in many ways around us.

In the image of Freyja reproduced here, which is based on a medieval wall-painting in Schleswig Cathedral in Germany, classical iconic conventions are followed. The goddess is shown full-faced. She carries a horn, multivalent symbol of summoning and plenty, emblem of the divine cow of Fe. Although she is blowing it, the iconographic conventions for a goddess followed by the artist at Schleswig mean that it does not obscure the divine face. Her ride on the tiger incorporates the wild elements of the hunter that honours the hunted beast in mystical rapport. It also recalls the cat as the *bid*, or sacred familiar animal of the witch. Freyja is the archetypal woman shamanic magician. She wears a talismanic amber necklace, Brisingamen. She flies with the use of a falcon-skin; she instructs the gods in the use of magic charms and the creation of potions; and she calls up magic fire. Her sybilline qualities, those she shares with Cybele, are recalled to this day local legends in Germany and Scandinavia.

To-day, Freyja is the symbol of human rapport with Nature. This comes not by attempting to command and control the natural world, but existing in an harmonious partnership, taking from Nature, but also giving to Nature. As personification of the Rune and Gothic letter, Freyja denotes the possession of power and strength without using it to dominate, abilities harnessed to necessity, which are not employed for a self-seeking, one-sided mastery over Nature and other sentient beings. In this Age of Representation, Freya is a reminder that post-modernity, in which the world is name resembles 'Ur', rides on a white bull, and in Germanic Paganism, one of the Valkyries, the female 'choosers of the slain', appeared in the form of a "fierce cow", an Aurochs. The Gothic letter Uraz also signifies primal strength, the force necessary for creativity. Perseverance and flow are combined to produce useful things, as in human handicrafts.

3. Thauris (Th, Þ), Defence,
(July 29 - August 12)

Thauris (Þ orn) is sacred to the goddess Thrud, (whose name means 'power-strength'). She is the counterpart of Thor, deity of Thrudheim ("The Place of Might"). Thauris's shape is a magical protection, representing the power of resistance against attack present in the thorn tree. This is achieved passively without a fight, by deterrence. The thorn contains the divine power which resists and repels everything threatening. Thauris is given in some texts as meaning a giant or troll, a being that terrifies all who see it. Folk-tradition tells of giants and trolls as guardians of certain places, resisting and repelling all who are foolhardy enough to dare to go there. Another aspect of Thorn is its ability to make a sudden change without warning.

Thauris's trees are the Blackthorn (*Prunus spinosa*), Hawthorn or May Tree (*Crataegus monogyna*), Bramble (*Rubus fruticosa*) and the Rose (*Rosa spp.*). The May Tree is the tree of the Goddess in her fertile aspect. The scent of its blossom recalls her most intimate secrets. Hawthorn and Blackthorn, and, to a lesser extent, Bramble and Rose, are plants used traditionally to make impenetrable hedges which enclose places both physically and magically.

Thauris's corresponding Gothic character, Thyth, signifies the Crystal Sphere, representing cosmic order. In the geocentric world-model, the Crystal Sphere represents the boundary between the material universe and the unseen world of divinity. In classical tradition, it is this sphere that is held by the giant Atlas. It denotes the eternal power of enclosure, a matrix that resists disorder and chaotic breakdown. In its form, the Gothic character is a hook that catches, an alternative representation of the runic thorn. Meditatively, this character brings the practical, functional, user's viewpoint.

Collectively, the first three characters of the Northern Alphabet denote different qualities of strength: Faihu is creative strength; Urus, the basic, earthy, collective strength; and Thauris, active bodily strength that wards of attack. The third and fourth characters describe two of the modes of vision that Alvis records in *Alvismal*: the third, Thauris-Thyth represents the giants' view, and the fourth, Ansus-Aza, signifies the godly one.

4. Ansus (A), the Goddesses and Gods of Order
(August 13 - August 28)

Ansus is the ancestral rune that denotes human descent from divine beings. Known as the 'goddess-' or 'god-rune', Ansuz is the fourth stave of the Elder Futhark. (Its other names are As, Aesc, Asa, and, as a variant form, Os). It is sacred to the gods and goddesses of civilised order. Ansus signifies the divine breath, önd, which, emanating from the divine sphere of Thauris, powers existence, the divine source within the human being. It is a powerful controller of the consciousness and all intellectual activities, reinforcing the divine order of existence. As is the rune of the Ash tree (*Fraxinus excelsior*). This is the cosmic axis linking the worlds, Irminsul or Yggdrassil, symbolic of order and stability. The parallel Gothic letter Aza represents the divine power of creation, interpreted according to Arian tradition as the energy of the Father God. It invokes the abundance and fecundity coming from divine blessings. Meditatively, this character brings the poetic, descriptive viewpoint of the gods.

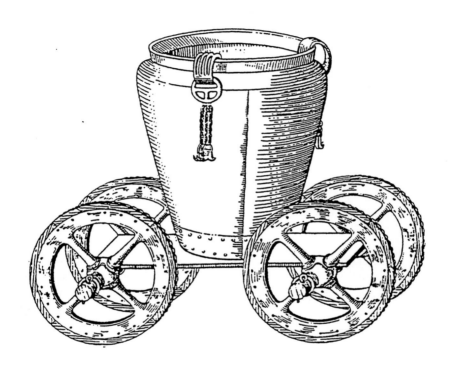

21. 'Cult Wagon' of the Hallstatt period (c. 1000 BCE), which is the archetype of the 'cauldron on the wagon', an archetype of the character Raida - Reda.

5. Raida (R), Motion,
(August 29 - September 12)

Raida is the fifth rune, whose sound is 'R'. As a divine rune, Raida represents the Sun-Wheel and Moon-Wheel, sacred to wheel-goddesses and gods, deities of roads and processes. Its name recalls Re, the Irish Moon-goddess of Emania, the otherworld. Other archetypal aspects of Raida are the Welsh goddess Arianrhod of the Silver Wheel, the Slovakian goddess Uroda and the Latin Fortuna, goddess of destiny, invoked to-day by card- and lottery-players as Lady Luck.

Raida is the rune of ritual and process, as in the rolling ascending and descending of the Sun-Wheel and the phases of the Moon-Wheel. Consequently, it refers to things to do with duration: periods of time, intervals, ages. Its name Raida refers to the wheel of time and its motion, the vehicle it carries, the physical or figurative road along which it rolls, and the time it takes to make the journey. Thus, Raida signifies both the 'vehicle' used to achieve an objective, and also the process by which it is achieved. It is both the way forwards and the means to get there. In this aspect, it refers to the Goddess in the Wagon, Nerthus, and goddess of roads Elen, otherwise known in European Paganism as Vrou Elden, Elaine and Helen. In common with many European sacred statues, the Pagan Gothic images were carried around the country on a wagon.

During their migrations, the Goths were dependent upon their vehicles, which were their homes, their temples and their castles. The Goths travelled across the land in great convoys of wagons, horses and livestock. During times of danger on the move, wagons were lashed together to make enormous mobile fortresses. At night, and during prolonged stops, the wagons were arranged in circular, wheel-shaped defensive formations. In the Gothic system, the meanings of Raida incorporate these unique experiences of vehicular life.

22. The Great Goddess Cybele, here shown with her atteendant dragons, in the Swabian landscape near the sybilline holy mountain of the Teck, whose attendant hill, the Bolle, shown in the background, is crowned by a grove of pine trees, visible for miles around.

Raida is the red thread of Verdandi ("That Which is Becoming"), the Norn of the present. Red thread is used in magical workings of binding. Red is the essential colour of the work of mystical creation, which is accomplished by union and transmutation. There, two separate entities are combined and transformed into a third one, which did not exist before. A related aspect of this rune is fruitfulness, beneficial results achieved through proper process in its own proper time. Because, magically, Raida assists the transfer of spirit, matter or information from one place to another, we must be in the right place at the right time, doing the right thing. An important aspect of Raida is in the way that it denotes personal transformation. Magically, this character can help us to take conscious control of our lives. Rad is the rune of the sacred red earth of, among other places, Lemnos, Westfalia and Rutland, the source of fruitfulness. The corresponding Gothic stave Reda has the same meaning as Raida, but encapsulating also the feminine creative power of the Mother Goddess, Nerthus, bringing reproductive fruitfulness.

6. Kusma (C, K), Illumination,
(September 13 - September 27)

The sixth rune is called Kusma. It is ruled by the gods and goddesses of knowledge, learning, insight, remembrance and wisdom, Woden, Freyja, Snotra, Vör and Var. The rune's name refers to the blazing chip of pine-wood (*Kienspan*), used for lighting in former times. It was cut from the tree sacred to Cybele, deity of Sybils and oracles. Kusma represents both physical light in outer darkness, and the inner light of knowledge. As the pine wood burns, it is transformed into heat, light and ash. Another meaning of Kusma is an abscess, burn, sore or wound. This expresses the way that sometimes, injury or illness can bring unexpected personal enlightenment. Kusma therefore symbolises the mystery of transformation. It has the power to bring personal illumination from far-seeing into other realms. It is valuable in providing psychic energy, assisting our powers of regeneration, empowering all positive actions. Similarly, the Gothic letter Chosma signifies the dual phenomenon of illness and illumination. It is the transformative power of heat and light, the borderline between madness and genius. Chosma relates to the Greek concept of the Aeon, which is represented by two blazing torches. According to Mithraic symbolism, they are the two torches of the attendants of Mithras. One is raised aloft, symbolising life, whilst the other points downwards, signifying death, the end of life.

7. Giba (G), a Gift,
(September 28 - October 12)

Giba is the X-shaped sacred mark of Paganism. It is the the linking-rune that denotes connections between people or the divine. This is the rune of the Northern goddess Gefn,"The Bountiful Giver", who is paralleled in the classical tradition by Abundantia, also a ruler of the Gothic letter Faihu. She is the goddess of giving on a material level.

A gift brings symbolic unification through exchange. Giba signifies the unity of the giver and the recipient, creating a balance and a tangible link. Giba is the power that links us with other people, or human existence with the divine. The Gothic character Gewa is a gift. It denotes the act of giving, and the bond that is made between the donor and recipient. It is the fusion of human and godly powers, the magical fusion of two wills. In late Classical magic, this letter pertains to the Flamen, promoter of the sacrifice, which has the character of a gift from the world of human beings to the world of the goddesses and gods.

8. Winja (V, W), Joy,
(October 13 - October 27)

The final rune of the first aett is Winja, sacred to the goddess Frigg, the Faery Queen, the Queen of Elfland. In rune-symbolism, it has two meanings. In the Gothic tradition, it is the pasture in which contented animals graze, in harmony with the world. More generally, it represents a flag, and signifies joy, the elusive condition of harmony amid a chaotic world.

Winja has a passive, indicative form as a flag or wind vane, and an active, generative one as a fan. It is that which denotes which of the eight winds is blowing, and therefore the atmosphere of here and now. In medieval times, women made the banners which warriors carried in battle. For instance, the daughters of the Norse viking Ragnar Lodbrok, one of the Pagan Martyrs, embroidered his famous 'luck-flag', the Raven Banner. The magic kerchiefs which medieval ladies gave to knights as favours, such as that given by Elaine to Lancelot, promised joy in victory and further joys of love-making on the warrior's triumphant return. We can find joy by living in balance with the world, like the flag which moves in concord with the winds.

Winja is the balance-point between the opposites. It transcends alienation and anxiety, whether they are caused by shortage or excess. It is a rune of fellowship, shared aims and general well-being. Magically, the Wyn-rune helps us to realise our true will. Then we can use it to fulfil our wishes and desires. Similarly, the Gothic letter Winne represents joy, the mystery of harmonious balance amid chaos. It is the mid-point between the opposites, a place of harmony, comfort, well-being and fellowship.

The Second Aett

9. Hagl (H), Constraint,
(October 28 - November 12)

The second aett, is ruled over by Hagl, the hailstone. It is the rune of wise women's craft, bringing transformation through consecration. The hailstone is a symbol of order and transformation. It falls from the sky as a hard, solid, crystalline mass which can do physical damage to anything it hits. Then, it melts into fluid, beneficial water. Hagl is connected deeply with women's worship and magic. Sacred to the goddess Holda, Hecate and Hela in their aspects collectively as The Hag, it is the rune of the Heathen priestesses of Pagan Holland, the Hagadissae, and the Hagazussa, the Moon priestesses of Germany, who practised until the 16th century. In modern times, as the traditional sigil of Juno, it has been called the 'hex sign'. In its female aspect, Hagl it is the rune of the Hagi, the grove of sacred trees. As the ninth rune, Hagl carries the most powerful sacred number of the Northern Tradition, "by the power of three times three".

There are variant forms of Hagl. In the Elder Futhark, it is like the Roman letter H, but in the Younger Futhark and modern Germanic runes, it is like a six-branched 'star'. The former Hagl represents the framework of the Loom of Existence, upon which the Web of Wyrd is woven, whilst the latter symbolises the crystalline primal seed, the basic geometry underling the structure of the material universe. It is the underlying nature of the processes which have to occur for anything to have being. The early Christian sigil called Chi-Rho, composed of the Greek letters for Ch and R, is also a version of this rune, binding it with the previous character, Winja.

Magically, Hagl was and is employed in warding- and binding-magic. It may be used as the bringer of confusion, disruption and chaos. But it is not only destructive: this activity is a necessary part of existence, expressing those patterns of events in our past life which have made the present state of things. The power of the goddess can make known to us those patterns originating in the past which are active in and affect the present. Hagal is the power of evolution within the framework of present existence.

On a personal level, Hagl is the rune of the unconscious mind and of the formative processes of thought. Transpersonally, it signifies the underlying structure of of things, both in terms of matter and time. Urd, "That Which Was" is the ruler of this aspect. It forms the psychic link between the non-material realms and Middle Earth. In this aspect, it is ruled by the goddesses who guard the passages that link the world of human consciousness with other planes: Mordgud, guardianess of the the icy bridge to the underworld, and Iduna, bringer of the Apples of Immortality. The Gothic character Haal is also the hailstone, the icy, primal seed of manifestation. It is the power of rapid and complete transformation from one state to another. Antique classical magic also links the Gothic letter with *Hyalus*, glass-green colour, and, by association, glass itself, which is structurally, if not chemically, related to ice. It is the stave of the mystical otherworldly Glass Castle of mythology.

The three runes at the beginning of this aett are icy and binding runes, expressing their place at the first part of winter in the year-circle.

10. Nauths (N), Necessity,
(November 13 - November 27)

Nauths is the rune of Nott, goddess of the dark night, who is the northern equivalent of the Egyptian goddess Nut. The

23. The sacred nail is an image of the character Eis - Iiz. These late
classical nails were used in holy binding-magic.

shape of the rune represents the two baulks of timber once used for making the magical need-fire. In former times, when famine or pestilence scathed the land, a fire was lit ritually to summon the assistance of the Goddess. The rune that represents this appeal means need. This refers both to an absence or scarcity of something, and also 'necessity'. Need is constraint, but within constraint the Goddess gives us the power to be released from that need. It reflects the maxim of the creatrix, "Lux e Tenebris", "From Darkness, Light".

Nauths emphasises the cyclic nature of all things. There are times of shortage and times of plenty: so we should not attempt to strive against our Wyrd, but try to use it constructively. We can see this in another of Nauth's deities: Skuld, the norn of the future, whose thread, black as night, binds all in the finality of death. Its main use in magic is for defensive binding spells, tying up psychic attack and disempowering opponents. The Gothic stave, Noics, also represents necessity and need. It is encapsulated in the archetype of the Old Woman. This contains within itself the means of release from that need, if we can recognise it. In Roman tradition, this letter signifies Justitia, the letter of justice, representing the name of the Roman goddess of destiny, Necessitas. She is also the goddess known as Nox or Hecate.

11. Eis (I), Stasis,
(November 28 - December 12)

In its form, the runic character Eis, and the Gothic letter Iiz is a vertical, fixed icicle. It stands for unchanging existence, the eternal present, and the element Ice. Ice is water that has changed in state from liquid to solid, through energy loss. By freezing, water becomes crystalline and resistant instead of flowing. The ice-rune therefore represents stopped activity. It is the rune of Rinda or Hrinda, goddess of the frozen earth. Also, because it represents the fixed present, it is the rune of

Verdandi, ("That which is eternally becoming"), the middle Norn.

But Eis and Iiz do not only represent motionlessness. Ice is usually static, but it can move under the right conditions. When it does, as in a glacier or iceberg, it moves imperceptibly slowly but with irresistible force. Thus, used magically, or appearing in a divination, the character delays or halts a process. It is the force of gravity, inertia, entropy and the cessation of activity. It is the process of inexorable destiny. Iiz is linked with the Greek deity, Kronos, the god with a cold character, who was called on by late antique magicians especially in their spells, to make their enemies cold, by bringing death.

12. Jer (J, Y), Year,
(December 13 - December 27)

The rune Jer and the Gothic character, Gaar, meaning 'year' or 'season' is the stave of Nature's cycles, symbolising completion at the proper time. The rune has two variants: an open form representing the waxing and waning moons, or the sickles of harvest-time. Gaar is even closer to the sickle in its form. These waxing and waning aspects of the moon are reconciled in the Full Moon, which is portrayed by the upright, stave-form of the rune. It is the rune of the goddesses of fertility, Freyja and Frigg, and of the harvest, Fulla or Ceres, and Libera, Roman goddess of fruitfulness.

Jer and Gaar symbolise a plentiful and rewarding harvest, which comes into being only in the right conditions, when appropriate actions have been taken, according to correct principles. In this, Jera denotes the natural order of things.

Jer's two basic forms are quite different from one another. The first has a standard upright stave, overlain by a circle or the diamond-shaped Iggws Ing-rune. This symbolises the stable state once it has been achieved. It represents the cosmic axis surrounded by the four seasons, a harvest garland with its supporting pole. In the runic year, it signifies the completion of the cycle, marking the winter solstice, the end of the old year and the beginning of the new. The second form consists of two angled staves, interpenetrating each another without touching. This is the dynamic form of Jer, representing progress towards completion.

13. Aihs (EO), Yew Tree, Bow, Pot-hook,
(December 29 - January 12)

Aihs is the thirteenth rune. It has two meanings, one in the realm of wood, and another in the realm of iron. In its wooden form, it is a stave cut from a Yew tree: the double-ended stave of life and death. In the days before firearms, a branch of Yew made the best bow. As a creator of weapons, bringing death at a distance, the Yew was a valuable but dangerous tree. In northern European tradition, the Yew is the tree of life and death because although it lives longest of all trees native to Europe, and is green throughout the year, its bark, leaves, roots, fruit and resin are all extremely poisonous. Because of this, Aihs is sometimes called the 'death rune'. Yews also possess exceptional powers of regeneration. Sometimes, an ancient Yews which is almost dead is regenerated by its own daughter tree which grows in the soil made inside its decaying trunk. Other Yews have never-healing wounds, from which the which red resin flows in an unceasing stream like menstrual blood. These 'Bleeding Yews' are sacred objects of pilgrimage.

The wooden form of Aihs is ruled by Skadi, the warrior destroyer-goddess of death and winter, and Ulli, god of the yew bow and skis, which were also made from the wood by traditional craftsmen. She presides over the season of Yule, the 'yoke' between the old and new years, affirming the power of Aihus for continuity and endurance. An important use for Yew is in magic runic staves that banish all harm, especially

24. An ancient Greek Lekythos showing a priest or Hermes conducting the *Pithoigia,* the jar-opening ceremony, where the spirits of the dead were released into the world for a little while, at the right time. After this, they return to the underworld of the jar. The related legend of Pandora seems to tell of an opening by the wrong person at the wrong time, releasing demonic forces into the realm of the living.

the powers of destruction and death. In their heyday, the Goths were formidable bowmen, fighting mainly as foot archers. Hence the significance of the bow in their culture. Weaving-stays were also made of Yew because of the physical-magical property of the wood. All staves, like the weaving-stay are used to impose the will upon the weft and warp of the material. It works both on the physical and non-material planes.

In its iron form, Aihs is the pot-hook, from which the cauldron was suspended over the fire. Throughout Europe, the pot-hook is regarded as the seat of the guardian spirit of the house which lives, literally, at its centre, magically protecting the inhabitants from physical and psychic harm. The pot-hook was used in weather-magic, for it was customary in many lands to take it outside the house in bad weather to dispel storms. In this aspect, it is a rune of binding. The equivalent Gothic letter, Waer, denotes the quality of sacrifice, giving up something valued in order to achieve an objective in return. For example, when the archer looses an arrow from his bow, he loses the valuable arrow in order that it may hit its target, whose form is reflected in the shape of the Gothic character.

14. Pairthra (P), a Pot, the Womb,
(January 13 - January 27)

The fourteenth rune is Pairthra. In its female aspect, it represents a pot, and, by correspondence, the womb. The rune's name may derive from the Greek word for a holy pot, used for pouring out blessings, and as a container of souls, the ΠθΟΣ (*Pithos*). Traditionally, pots and vases were women's work, where the clay of Mother Earth was made into symbolic wombs of the Earth Mother. Mythologically, it is the the vessel which receives corpses to regenerate them, such as the cauldrons buried with central European dignitaries from the Hallstatt period onwards.

In Celtic mythology, the Cauldron of Cerridwen represents the symbol of rebirth through the goddess. The womb of woman is the archetypal Pairthra, the port or gateway into life. The male interpretation of this rune, the only one usually discussed, is the dice-cup, dispenser of fate through chance. This refers to the Law of the Unity of Opposites present in all gifts.

Pairthra represents the womb of the Great Goddess, Allmother, She who brings all things into physical existence. In the Greek tradition, from which the Gothic takes certain elements, the *Pithos* was used to bury the dead. In ancient Greece, at certain times of year, the burial pots were opened so that the spirits of the dead could return to this plane for a little while. Also, the jar signifies the *Pithogia* of Pandora, who, in opening the jar, let the world's ills loose amongst humankind. Pairthra thus uncovers previously concealed things. It is the power of Wyrd in the world, bringing forth its potential into physical manifestation. Pairthra symbolises the interplay between the freedom of our conscious will-power and the constraints of our surrounding conditions. In the game of life, the pattern of the board and the rules of movement of the gamepieces are already laid down. But, beyond these limitations, our actions are free. They are the result of our personal skill and conscious will, interacting with our surrounding conditions. We have free will within the constraints of our own Wyrd. The cynic philosopher Diogenes chose to live 'the life of a jar' as a practical example of his beliefs.

On a practical level, Pairthra is connected with memory and recollection, problem-solving and esoteric knowledge. It provides access to the inner secrets of thins, both in the human world and also to wider Nature. Through Pairthra, we are given the ability to distinguish the valuable from the worthless, giving meaningful insights into otherwise puzzling inner experiences. The Gothic character Pertra is obliquely related to the runic meaning. Pertra is the brilliant Solar Halo that signifies the irresistible processes of Nature that can bring unexpected benefits out of difficult situations.

15. Algs (Z), The Elk, Guardianship,
(January 28 - February 11)

Algs (Eiwaz), whose shape symbolises the awesome power of the Elk, is the magically-powerful defensive rune of the Disir, the Divine Grandmothers (Fairy Godmothers, Personal Guardian Spirits), rulers of time-keeping. Magically, Algs is the most powerful defensive rune of personal protection. Visualising the rune around oneself invokes one's guardian spirit, as a protection against all kinds of physical and psychic attack It counters all harmful forces and influences, known and unknown, which conflict with us. It gives us assistance in attempting to obtain divine qualities. This rune is also a Lappish constellation, Sary, the Elk, known as Orion in classical western astrology.

The related Gothic character Ezec represents the Fifteen Stars of traditional European astronomy. The Fifteen Stars are the fixed time-markers that serve as a bridge between the human and the divine. The Fifteen Stars are actually single stars and asterisms. They were important in navigation on sea and land, and some of them served as markers for the calendar. They are Alcyone (of the Pleiades), Arcturus, Antares, Aldebaran, Capella, Deneb Algedi, Sirius, Regulus, Polaris, Alphecca, Algorab, Vega, Algol, Procyon and Spica. They are the most significant fixed stars in astrology, being ascribed specific characters that can be used to read the planetary influences. Readers can find further details of the correspondences of the Fifteen Stars in the author's book, Runic Astrology (Capall Bann, 1995).

A work on electional astrology for use of apprentices in The Honourable Guild of Locators, now in preparation, will deal with this tradition and the Fifteen Stars in greater detail.

25. The Sun, fountain of light, personified by Helios, Apollo and the Christ. Tarot trump XIX from Nigel Pennick's *Way of the Eight Winds Tarot*.

16. Saúil (S), Sun,
(February 12 - February 26)

The last rune of the second aett is Saúil, the rune of the Sun. In its female aspect, Sigel is ruled over by the solar divinity of the North, the goddess Saúil (called Saule in Lithuania and Phoebe in East Anglia). It draws in the illuminating, healing and nurturing power of the morning sun's rays, helping us to achieve our full potential. Saúil, grandmother sun, 'the glory of Elves', is known in the Celtic tradition as Grainne. The rune Saúil, is in the form of the emblem of the goddess Súúle, the sun reflected on water. Drawing upon the power of the sun, the rune counters the forces of death and disintegration, heralding the triumph of light over darkness in the period of the rising light.

The Gothic stave Sugil is also representative of the stupendous power of the sun, both physically and spiritually. It is the embodiment of magical will, the harbinger of victory, and the ascendancy of light over darkness. It is seen in the Gothic alphabet as male, reflecting the Christian mystical tradition of the sun being both representative of the Christ and also the embodiment of St Michael. But its Greek roots lie in the Pagan sigil Planeta, which refers to both sun and moon, Helios and Selene.

The Third Aett

17. Teiws
(February 27 - March 13)

Teiws is the first rune of the third aett, the Aett of Teiwaz and Zisa. Tiewaz is the old European sky god, who appears under different names in different parts of our continent. The goddess Zisa is the equivalent of the Roman goddess Juno, (Juno Regina) queen of heaven, protectress of every woman

26. Gothic emblems of victory, relating to the Great God Termagant, equivalent to the god Mars worshipped by the ancient Goths.

through life, from birth to death; and the three-breasted Celtic goddess Gwen Tierbron. Her festival, the Matronalia (March 1) is in the half-month of the rune Teiws.

The female version of this rune represents the cosmic pillar of heaven, Irminsul. This signifies a rune of being in the correct place at the correct time for the greatest effect. It is universal figure, being a version of the ancient Egyptian Ankh and the Coptic Christian Tau cross, manifested in central Europe as the pillar Irminsul, whose form is that of a palm tree. Teiws signifies positive regulation and successful achievement of objectives are the function of this rune. The Gothic letter Tyz has a related meaning. Tyz represents earthly, human, power, victory and achievement on the material plane. It is primarily the stave of human male power, and is thus associated with the warlike, masculine archetype as represented by Quirinus, Mars, Termagant and Tîwaz, the deity most associated with the Pagan Goths. The Throne of Majesty symbolises this character.

18. Baírkana (B),
Birch, (March 14 - March 29)

Representing the Birch tree (*Betula pendula*), is Baírkana, symbol of birth and regeneration. The Birch was the first tree to recolonise the treeless land at the end of the last Ice Age. Its shape resembles the breasts of the Great Mother, Nerthus, symbolising nurture. It is the birth-rune, a rune of new beginnings. Its number, 18, represents completion, and new beginnings on a higher, organic, level. Primal laws have been defined, and the next stage of growth can commence. Baírkana is a rune of purification and new beginnings, most sacred to female magic: it clears away earlier influences, allowing new ones to be created.

Traditionally, the 'brush' part of the witch's broomstick is made of birch twigs. The Gothic character Bercna is similarly a

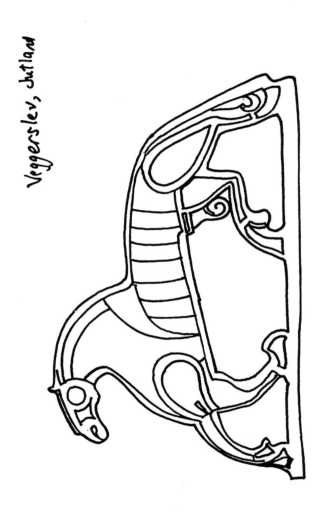

Veggerslev, Jutland

27. The horse, symbol of movement. A stone-carving at Veggerslev, Jutland, Denmark, the homeland of the Heruli.

symbol of completion and regeneration, as manifested in the Birch tree. Symbolically, it represents the human female power.

Another aspect of Baírcana-Bercna is in the archaic bear cult of the north, the background of the warrior tradition that originated in hunting magic. The enormous power of growth of the Birch is reflected in the awesome power of the bear as a predatory animal. In Scandinavia, he who wore a shirt of bear skin was a *Berserker*, a ferocious practitioner of the martial arts who went without normal chain-mail armour, yet who was so terrifyingly strong that he struck fear into his adversaries. These bear-warriors "went without mail byrnies (mail shirts), as ferocious as dogs or wolves" records *The Ynglinga Saga*, "they bit their shields and were as strong as bears or boars; they killed men, but neither fire nor iron could hurt them. This is called 'running berserk'..." The bearskin shirt was the heraldic emblem that gave the bear-warrior the ability to draw upon the power of the bear in battle. The cult of the bear was widespread throughout the northern hemisphere, from Siberia, across northern Europe to North America. As his initiation, the bear-warrior had to kill a bear and drink its blood. Then the warrior gained 'bear's strength', and the power of the bear was his.

19. Egeis (E), Horse,
(30 March - 13 April)

Egeis is the rune of one of the most sacred animals of Heathen Europe, used in divination, shamanism and royal pageantry. The goddesses of the horse-rune are Freyja and Epona. Egeis represents the horse-shoe, the cunnic symbol of the goddess. It is the rune of combination, like the horse and rider, bringing things together into an unbreakable bond. Egeis represents the partnership of the will and the physical necessities we need to create any positive movement. On a psychic level, it is the seer's journey, for the horse is the sacred animal of Odin, the Hoodening Horse. The seer's journey into other areas of existence links Egeis with the Gothic stave Eyz, which signifies the Aether, the cosmic medium that pervades the universe. It is a character of combination, the necessity for a medium that the information may be transmitted, on a human level, partnership. Eyz represents önd, the empowering 'cosmic breath' that is utilised by geomants, diviners and practitioners of the martial arts alike.

20. Mannaz (M), Human Being,
(April 14 - April 28)

The rune Mannaz denotes the basic qualities of humanness that we all have, whether we are female or male. European tradition asserts that human beings originated as from trees. A Norse myth tells that Askr, the first man, came from an Ash tree (*Fraxinus excelsior*), and Embla, the first woman, from an Elm (*Ulmus procera*). Similarly, the Celtic Bards assert that the first woman was a Rowan tree (*Sorbus acuparia*), and the first woman an Alder tree (*Alnus glutinosa*). Man signifies our common human experience as daughters and sons of Mother Earth. This rune has a shape that reflects the archetypal human being. On a collective level, it is a symbolic embodiment of human social order, without which we cannot achieve our full human potential. Because language is the primary human quality, Man is a Hogrune (a rune of the mind). In meditation, this stave enhances the human viewpoint of the thirteen parts of the world as expounded in *Alvismal*. The Gothic stave Manna represents the archetypal reality of man which exists in every human, male or female. It is the shared experience of every human being. It is also the trees, from which, in Nordic and Greek tradition, humans originated. The sacred images of the Pagan Goths were tree-trunks with godly heads carved at the top. Dressed in fine garments, they were paraded around the country periodically on wagons or camels.

21. Lagus (L), Flowing Water,
(April 29 - May 13)

Representing water in its many phases and moods are the rune Lagus and the Gothic letter Laaz. Primarily, they are characters that signify fluidity, denoting the flowing powers of the tides, the force of waterfalls, and the vigorous power of growth. They are the qualities of fluidity, mutability and the uncertainties of existence. It is power of organic growth, and action at a distance under the influence of the Moon. Organic increase proceeds in cycles, visible in the growth rings of trees and seashells. The power of Lagus and Laaz power helps to clear away things that delay proper progress, accelerating those flows of events which are already taking place. Lagus's qualities relate it to chthonic and watery deities, such as Nerthus. There is also lunar influence.

22. Iggws (Ng), Generative Energy,
(May 14 - May 28)

Iggws, the Ingrune, is the symbol of generative power. Iggws has two forms, of which the inward-looking, shaped like a 'diamond' is the female aspect. It is the yoni of the Goddess, containing the inner fire of creativity. The female Iggws-rune takes many forms: it is the yoni of the Mother Goddess, a place of fecundity: it is the Vesica Piscis, the origin-point of geometry; and the milrind at the centre of the millstone. As Ingvé and Ingeborg, it is the symbol of Nerthus. The Danish goddess Yngona has this symbol manifested in physical form in the vast cunnic-shaped stone enclosures of Lindholm HØje in Denmark.

In English heraldry, an unmarried woman entitled to a coat-of-arms in her own right has a shield in the shape of the Iggws-rune. The outgoing form, the Ingrune, expresses the power of the god Ing, an aspect of the phallic deity Freyr. Magically, Iggws is a channel for potential energy. It is a "doorway to the

28 Mother Earth, the goddess Fjörgynn.

astral". Similarly, the Gothic character Enguz denotes becoming, the eternal present. This is potential energy, that which must undergo a period of build-up before release as a single burst of power, such as an orgasm.

23. Othal (O), Earth, Home, Possession
(May 29 - June 13).

Othal is the *Eeyen-eerde* rune, meaning 'own earth' or 'own land', with the specific meaning of patrimony or inherited territory. It is primarily the rune of Erda (also manifesting as the goddesses Nerthus, Fjörgynn and Jörth), Mother Earth, whose symbol represents the heart of the land, and the hearth within of the home, its spiritual centre, locus of the house spirit. Othal's shape is an enclosure under human control. Good things can be kept there, safe from harm. It is the centre in which creative human activities can take place in safety and harmony. Othal maintains powerfully existing states, affirming our connections with other people in our group or family. It resists arbitrary rules, and preserves the liberty of human free will within the framework of Nature. The Gothic stave Utal likewise represents riches and abundance, the result of useful knowledge, wise decisions and proper conduct. It is our material and spiritual heritage. Meditatively, Othal-Utal brings the viewpoint of the dwarves, that of the detailed, precise, yet beautiful symbolic vision of existence.

Most fundamental to us all is the female principle of the Earth expressed by Othal-Utal. As the Earth-goddess, she is called many names in the European Pagan tradition: inter alia, Gaea, Tellus Mater, Erda, Nehalennia, Nerthus, Jör𐌗, Fjörgynn, Will's Mother and Zemyna. Throughout the world, in places where patriarchal monotheistic religion has not driven her veneration underground, she is acknowledged. Whether she is acknowledged or not, all life on this planet comes from the Earth Mother, and returns to her. Tirelessly, she nourishes plant, animal and human life. Without her, there could be no existence. In the Northern Tradition, she is personified as the Goddess Jörth. In another aspect, Fjörgynn, Mother Earth, she is mother of the goddess Frigg and the god Thor.

After the fall of the Roman Empire in western Europe, the female divine principle, acknowledged by the Pagans, was driven gradually underground, forbidden by theocratic governments. Of course, this deterred only the external forms of Goddess-awareness, whilst leaving the inner, secret, core relatively unaffected. Externally, the Goddess reasserted herself in the thirteenth century of the Common Era, when the worship of Mary, Mother of God became prominent in the western church. This was in response to the Crusaders' horror when they entered the Wasteland, the barren deserts of North Africa and the Middle East, which, according to Arab mystics, had come into being as the result of renouncing the Goddess there. The patriarchal, authoritarian cult of mastery, promoting the conquest of Nature, had destroyed the older, more nurturing, ecologically-sustaining, ways, replacing them with a destructive on-lay.

The salutary shock of encountering the Wasteland led to the setting-up of cults of more active female saints, themselves versions of female Pagan deities. Later, the secession of the Protestants from the western church led to a renewed suppression of female aspects of the divine. Images of the Madonna and female (and male) saints were destroyed. In central and southern Europe, however, the Roman Catholic Counter-Reformation gave the Madonna even more prominence. Many new shrines of the Mother of God were created, and the cult of the Black Madonna thrives to-day.

Like the deserts of North Africa and the Middle East, the modern polluted wastelands have also come about through the application of the theologies of command and control. These preach the transformation of the world into a re-presentation of reality patterned in the image of Man - an on-lay that stems in part from the renunciation of the Goddess. To those who brought this about, the Earth was no longer sacred, but only a meaningless object, a 'resource' to be used for the short-term profit of individuals. Through this misunderstanding of the nature of existence, a program to make the Earth barren was instituted. This unthinking dispossession of life is still continuing, although there is a growing awareness that it is not such a good idea after all. The image of the Goddess, wherever she exists, personified by this rune and Gothic letter, is symbolic of the spiritual resistance to this degrading and destructive principle.

24. Dags (D), Day,
(June 14 - June 28)

The final, rune of the Elder Futhark is Dags. It is paralleled by the Gothic letter Daz. Both Dags and Daz mean 'day'. The rune is the Northern Tradition symbol for the protection of entrances, invoking the power of the guardian goddess Syn. She maintains internal harmony and balance by allowing in only those things that are good or necessary, whilst excluding the harmful and unnecessary.

When used against harmful things, the Dags-rune is a powerful blocker. But for beneficial things, it is a rune of openings, light, health and prosperity. When woven into fabric, painted or carved on openings in the house, it does the work of Syn, preventing entry of harmful sprites and önd, whilst admitting things which are desirable. Dags is also the rune of invisibility. Things, and people, protected by Syn's rune are not noticed. The corresponding Gothic stave, Daz, signifies day, light and awakening, strength bringing joy. It is the archetype of wholeness, the fourfold Holy City or Paradise Garden that reconciles the necessary polarities of existence.

25. Quairtra (Q), Cosmic Fire, Quintessence,
(the whole year).

The final Gothic character, Quairtra, represents the swirling flames of the ceremonial fire, which does not have the normal properties of the ordinary element of fire. It signifies complete cleansing by the transmutation of things from one form to another. Quairtra has no Gothic rune parallel, but it is equivalent to the Northumbrian rune Cweorth, with which it never came into contact until modern times. As the cosmic fire, Quairtra is the fifth element or Quintessence of alchemy, which is another way of describing the Nwyvre of Northern Tradition. Thus, it is outside the realm of the other 24 characters, encapsulating and incorporating the essence of each and every one. Because of this, Quairtra is not included within the circle of 24, and occupies at once both the centre and circumference of the circle.

Chapter 6
Techniques of Gothic Divination

The earliest recorded technique of rune-reading tells that slivers of wood marked with characters were cast upon a cloth. From this comes the expression "casting the runes". A similar technique was used by the Greeks, who threw the sheep knuckle-bones called *astragali* in a ceremonial manner. The patterns they formed gave the divinatory reading. Sometimes, the *astragali* were marked in some way, with letters or dots like dice, and indeed, they may be the origin of dice.

Significantly, Icelandic folklore ascribed the invention of both the runes and of dice to Odin. Like the runes, dice originated as a technique of divination. They are related to numerical and combinatorial oracles like divinatory geomancy (for details of which see my *The Oracle of Geomancy*, Capall Bann, 1995). Although at one time, the runes were cast, developments in technique means that to-day there are many other possibilities of using symbolic letters in divination. There are two basic forms that can be used. Either the letters or runes are carved or drawn upon stones, or some form of cards can be made. Either kind lend themselves to the following methods.

The most basic way of choosing a rune or Gothic character is simply to take one stone from a bag, or to pull one card from the deck. This gives an instant reading which has the merit of being spontaneous but the drawback that any negative thoughts, states of mind, or surrounding conditions will inevitably be apparent. As in all traditional systems of divination, it is far more desirable to conduct a divination in a

29. The Gothic Alphabet.

f u th a r k g w h n

i j z p x s t b e m

l ng o d q

divination, it is far more desirable to conduct a divination in a ceremonial manner. When we cast the characters ceremonially, then we must be mindful of the diviner's location and the direction in which the divination is to be made before we conduct the ceremony. Most importantly is to be in a proper frame of mind, free of preoccupations and distractions, whilst conducting a divination,

A useful ceremonial technique of Gothic divination is known as *Raed Waen*, 'riding the wagon'. In this technique, the diviner places him- or herself metaphorically in the position of the god or goddess on the wagon, from which all things can be seen. 'Riding the wagon' is a divinatory rite in which the actual casting, the *shoat* or 'shoot' is carried out. When we conduct the ceremony of *Raed Waen*, we always take into account the surrounding physical and psychic environment. As with any activity which requires harmony with prevailing conditions, it is necessary be aware of their effects upon the proceedings.

When we choose to conduct *Raed Waen* indoors, then the axis of the shoat should coincide with the main axis of the room - the *rig* or *right line*. This can be visualized as an imaginary straight line drawn across the floor. It need not be accurate in surveying terms, and so can be worked out easily. Theoretically, the right line should be the alignment which is best in harmony with the energies of the Earth in that room, and is therefore an aspect of the ancient art of location. In a building where the walls are oriented correctly, that is, facing the four cardinal directions, the axis should lie in the direction east-west. In the Northern Tradition, this is the direction of non-adversarial interactions, lying at right-angles to the *presence*, which is the place of the gods which is located in the north.

In the Northern Tradition, the adversarial orientation has the 'plaintiff' facing northwards to be judged by the judge, who him or her faces southwards at the 'presence' in the north. But as in all areas of locational practice, practicality must be the

30. The Circle of the Year. The runes, time and the eight winds.

the east-west axis, then the rig should be laid out parallel to the longer wall, dividing the floor space into two parts.

Once the line has been determined, then, the *shoat* itself can be aligned along this axial rig. The shoat is a casting cloth whose dimensions should be taken from the bodily dimensions of the diviner. This measure is the diviner's own 'length' from his or her feet to the finger-tips, when they are held at full stretch above the head. The cloth's width should be identical with the distance between the diviner's outstretched arms, measured from fingertip to fingertip. This is the traditional measure of the personal Fathom. Of course, the cloth should be made ceremonially well in advance of the time it is needed for divination. When a divination is to be made, we place the cloth on the floor in such a way that its central point is located one-third of the way along the right line. Ideally, the view of the diviner is thus along the longer part of the room. The wall in front of the diviner then becomes positive, and the wall behind her or him, negative. Proper orientation according to the traditional European principles of the Honourable Guild of Locators means that east is positive, west negative, with the *presence* north to the left and south to the right. From the enquirer's viewpoint, the direction along the rig towards the positive wall is considered 'up', and that nearer to the diviner, 'down'. 'Left' and 'right' refer to the diviner's actual left and right.

Out of doors, Gothic divination has two orientational principles. It is possible either to do an orientation by the sun, as described below, or to align the shoat towards the holy island of Gotland, the spiritual homeland of the Goths. This ancestral island lies in the Baltic sea to the east of Sweden. Its geographical location is 57° 30' N., 18° 30' E., approximately. Use a map if necessary. By orientating towards Gotland, we can partake of the spiritual qualities of the sacred land when we use the Gothic technique. Alternatively, we can orientate the right line should towards the Sun at the time that we are performing the ceremony. According to traditional belief, human energy flows towards the Sun, whilst the Sun's energy comes towards us in a complementary manner. Naturally, this direction is changing continuously, and its actual orientation depends on the time of day. At true midday, the Sun stands due south, and at midnight, though it invisible to us 'beneath the Earth', it stands at due north. The other times of day and night have their own proper solar orientation, with the Sun appearing to complete a whole cycle in 24 hours. In the Northern Tradition correspondence used here, each of these 24 hours corresponds with one of the 24 Gothic runes, and the first 24 Gothic letters. Only the Gothic character Quairtra is outside and beyond the cycle.

We can visualise this whole character-circle if we think of ourselves standing inside a circular building with a series of 24 stained-glass windows all around us. Each of the windows is filled with radiant glass depicting one of the Gothic characters in its appropriate position. Each occupies one twenty-fourth part of the circle. During the daylight hours, we could see the sun illuminating each character in its proper turn at the correct hour. This is because each character is located at a certain airt or compass-direction that corresponds with the direction of the sun at a specific hour of the 24-hour cycle.

The day cycle begins with the character Faihu - Fe. It commences at 12.30, and runs until 13.30. When we use local solar time, which is shown by a sundial, then the sun is in any one Gothic character-direction at its corresponding time of day. Correspondingly, the rune/character Jer - Gaar occupies the northernmost slot, whilst Dags - Daz is the most southerly. The character guarding the eastern airt is Baírkana - Bercna, whilst Kusma - Chosma stands as the representative of the west.

The other characters occupy their corresponding positions in the day circle. Each Gothic character-hour runs from the 'half before the 'hour' until the 'half' after it. Using the 24-hour clock, we can see that the character hour of Jer - Gaar begins clock, we can see that the character hour of Jer - Gaar begins at 23.30 hrs and is active until 00.30 hrs. The next character hour, Aihs - Waer, runs from 00.30 until 1.30, and so on. The final Gothic character hour in the circle, ruled by Dags - Daz, begins at 11.30 and ends at 12.30 hrs.

It is a general principle that, unless there are exceptional circumstances, it is undesirable to conduct divinations during the hours of darkness. According to Northern Tradition teachings, divinatory procedures should take place "In the face of the Sun, and the eye of the light". But when a divination must be carried out for a special reason in relation to a certain character and its corresponding direction, then it may have to be performed at night. This comes about because sometimes it is necessary to make the shoat in the direction of a specific character, and at the corresponding character-hour hour of the day or night. Then the rig that we use must face towards the apparent position of the sun, whether it is visible or not.

When we do a divination out of doors, we always remember to remove our shoes so that we make physical contact with the earth. Then we sit upon a cushion situated at the negative end. This is often be a ceremonial object embroidered with appropriate sigils to empower divinations. Such a cushion is called technically a *stol*. A personal talisman called the *mearomot* can be laid upon another, smaller, cloth at the positive end of the casting cloth. The *mearomot* can vary; it may be a talismanic pouch, a special stone, a crystal, shell, spirit-bird's feather or any other object which can assist the diviner on a non-material level. Whatever it is, it should embody something of diviner's own essence. Along with this talisman is the paper on which the question is written. In addition to the *mearomot,* the diviner should locate symbolic objects at the four corners of the shoat.

Once the arrangement of the ceremonial shoat has been completed, then the diviner performs personal ceremonies of personal composure and mental cleansing. Now, he or she will take some time for quietude and self-recollection. During this process, all bad, harmful, negative or distracting thoughts should be banished. Also, only the diviner, the querent and people with an interest in them should be present. A divination is not a show, and except when it is being taught to students, should never be conducted for an audience. Equally, 'tempters and deriders', those people who are negative influences upon the divination and the diviner, should be sent away. Indoors, the divination should not be performed under electric lighting, for the flickering of the alternating current adversely affects the consciousness of diviner and querent alike. It is best to perform the divination in daylight, or, when artificial lighting is an absolute necessity, by candle-light.

Only after all of these things have been arranged to the satisfaction of the diviner should the question then be asked. Before the question is drafted, the querent should think hard about it. Once it is formulated, then the question should be written out. Questions for Gothic divination should be expressed in straightforward, and not in ambiguous language. One question should refer to a single concept only, and avoid complex and muddled thought. Then both querent and diviner might meditate for a while on the meaning of the divination. But we must always bear in mind that, although they are an effective oracle, the Gothic staves cannot give an intelligible answer to an unintelligible question.

The next stage should be done when it feels appropriate. Shuffle the cards in the deck, or jumble the stones in the casting-bag. If we are using cards, then we cut the deck three times. Next, we take the cards or stones and lay them out in our chosen spread. There is a galster or formula that some diviners use when performing this act, saying, chaning or singing: "I seek guidance and light that I may live well". As you turn up each card and lay it on the shoat, you can say, "Read right!". Among other things, this helps to invoke the Gothic archetypes to give appropriate advice.

Some of the spreads given here are threefold. This reflects the triadic nature of the three Fates, which are recognized throughout the European spiritual tradition. In the Classical tradition, they are the Parcae or Moirae; in the Northern Tradition, they are the Norns or Weird Sisters. Whatever they are called, their actions underlay the nature of transvolution - the way things happen. In a Gothic divination, the first card or part of the spread relates to the first Fate, called in the Greek tradition, Clotho. She represents past events and actions which make up the present. The second card, stone or element relates to Lachesis the middle Fate. She is the present, eternal becoming. The last card or part is related to the third Fate, Atropos. She represents 'that which should become'.

The simplest multiple-character technique takes only three stones or cards. Each card or stone represents one of the Fates. The first (left-hand) card denotes the factors of the past that underlie the reading; the second (middle) signifies the present state of things; and the third (the right-hand one), denotes the result of the reading. The result given tells us what we can expect to be the outcome of the present situation, if we do not use free will to alter the outcome. It is important to recognise this. The Gothic reading tells us what potential outcome is likely, and under no circumstances should we view the result of a reading as indicating our unalterable fate.

The Grid of Nine

Because of the threefold nature of existence within time, it seems best to use spreads that have a threefold inner structure. A useful spread uses nine cards or stones, the most revered sacred number of the Northern Tradition, "by the power of three times three". The Grid of Nine, a square subdivided into nine smaller squares, is the form of the *Frithsplot* or sacred enclosure in Northern Tradition worship, magic and meditation. It is this grid that protects the threshold of the house as well as being the form used for the magical enclosure used in the technique of *Utiseta* (Sitting Out). In the Square of Nine divination, each aspect of the threefold structure of transvolution is broken down into three distinct stages. Each in turn are examined in terms of their aspects of beginning, process and termination or outcome. Thus the overall rulership of the lowest line of a nine-character shoat is under Clotho. It reads from left to right as: I, factors operating on the origin of past events; II, the process of those past events; and III, the result of those past events. The second (middle) line relates to the Fate called Lachesis. From left to right, it reads: IV, as the factors acting on the present as the result of card III; V, present processes; and VI, the results of that process which are being experienced now. The third (upper) line relates to the last Fate, Atropos. It refers to: VII, the changes coming from present conditions; VIII, the altered process of the changes; IX, the final outcome of those changes.

The Celtic Cross

This technique is best known as a Tarot spread, but it works equally well with the runes. The first part of the spread involves making the cross itself. Firstly, the diviner selects a card or stone to represent the querent, or the subject of the reading. It is best to use the Gothic character that corresponds with her or his birth-date, as listed in the appendix.

Alternatively, the character may be that which best represents the subject in question. Thus, a question about money would have Faihu - Fe as its significator, or one about human concerns and relationships would take Mannaz - Manna. This significator is laid facing upwards on the casting cloth. Then the rest of the deck must be shuffled, or the stones tumbled in the bag. Then, the first stave will be turned up, and placed over the significator, thereby covering the character that represents the querent. This stave denotes the general influences that are acting upon the question, and also the general conditions that prevail concerning it. The second stave (I) 'crosses' the querent stave. The diviner places it sideways across the first one. It is customary to read this character as upright, no matter which way it falls, whereas some diviners believe that should a character appear upside down, this denotes the reversal of its meaning. The second stave represents those forces that are hindering or opposing the questioner.

Next, the third character (stone or card II) is laid 'beneath' the questioner's stone. This one indicates the underlying influences and processes that are operating at the most basic level, that is the querent's own personal experiences of the matter under consideration. The diviner puts down the next character (III) to the left of the significator, 'behind' the querent's stave. This stave shows the influence which is passing away now, or has just ended. The next card or stone (IV) 'crowns' the significator, as it is placed immediately above it. This expresses any new influences which are likely to come into being in the medium to long term. The next stone or card (V) is laid to the right of the significator, 'before' it. This indicates the influences which may be acting upon the querent in the immediate future.

By now, the staves are arranged in a cruciform pattern, the Celtic Cross itself. The first part of the spread is completed now, but there is still more to, come. The second part of the spread involves erecting a column of four more stones or cards. These are turned up, and laid, in order, starting at the bottom and working upwards. The bottom, card or stave (VI), represents all of the negative feelings and fears present in the querent.

The second columnar stave (VII), laid down above the previous one, denotes the immediate environment of the questioner. More specifically, it refers to the various influences of friends and relatives. The next stave (VIII) stands for the questioner's hopes and beliefs concerning the question. Finally, at the top of the column, stave (IX) denotes the likely final outcome of the matter in question, which is the summation of the the influences delineated by the other nine cards.

The Ninefold Spread

This method also has its origins in Tarot-reading. It is in effect a variant of the Celtic Cross spread detailed above. It differs from the to the Celtic Cross in that the second card is not used. In the Celtic Cross spread, the second card signifies the immediate influences that are acting upon the questioner. The meaning of the other slivers, stones or cards in the Ninefold Spread are identical with those in the Celtic Cross.

The Cosmic Axis Spread

The final spread recommended here has eleven cards. It is similar to the previous one, but includes two further cards which represent the conceptual cosmic axis. This is the vertical axial line that links the three psychic levels within the human being, projected outwards onto the world as a geocentric model of the cosmos. At the base of the cosmic axis is the Underworld (known in the Norse tradition as Utgard and in the Greek as Hades), the place of lower forms of existence, where lost souls are repurified for rebirth once more upon the next level up. This next level, above Utgard - Hades, is the Middle World, the Earth on which we live, called Midgard or Gaea. Above this, the axis links us with the Upperworld, Asgard or the Empyrean. For further details of the mythos and structure of the cosmic axis, see Nigel Pennick's *The Cosmic Axis* (Runestaff, 1985).

The cosmic axis spread can be viewed as a development of the Grid of Nine spread, providing, however, additional information. To make this spread, the cards or stones are randomised in the usual manner, and then laid out on the casting cloth. If we choose to, we may use a significator, as in the Celtic Cross spread, but this is not strictly necessary. When we use one, we lay it at the central point of the spread, the *Nowl*, at the very centre of the shoat. Whether or not we use a significator, we place the first stave of the spread proper at the base of the central column. This is followed by one card or stone to the left, and another to the right of it; together, these three characters create the lower tier of the cosmic axis, Hades or Utgard. The next card or stone is a linking stave. It is laid directly above the first card. Then another, the fifth, character, is placed directly above this. It lies on top of and 'crosses' the significator if one is used.

We follow this central stave by creating the central, Midgard, level in the same way as the lower tier. One stave is placed to the left, and another to the right, of the middle one. The next step comes when we place another stave above the middle one. This is the second linking character, the upper part of the axis proper. Then we put a further stone or card above it. This is the central character of the upper level of the cosmic axis. Completion of the spread comes when a further card or stone is placed to the left and to the right of it. In all, eleven staves have been used, twelve if we include a significator.

There are two ways that we can interpret this cosmic axis spread.his spread can be interpreted in two ways. The more common interpretation uses the lower tier to represent the past. The central card of this level signifies the major influences that have affected the querent in the past. To the left is the questioner's subconscious response to this influence, and to the right is her or his conscious. Above this, the linking rune denotes the outcome of these influences which have led to the present condition. This is the Gothic character directly above the lower axis, the central stave lying over the significator if used used. The left-hand stave on this, the level representing present effects, specifies the subconscious influences that are acting at the present time.

Correspondingly, the letter to the right of the centre informs us of the conscious influences present now. Above this central stone or card, the upper link details the result that these present influences will bring if nothing is done to change the situation. And directly above this one, the upper tier of the cosmic axis signifies the likely outcome of events. The central card of the top level denotes the major apparent result of the process, with the subconscious effect to its left and the consciously-perceived effect to its right.

An alternative interpretation can be made, where the cosmic axis is viewed as a real structure, as it is portrayed in Northern Tradition spirituality. Here, the lower tier is the abyss or underworld, the realm of unformed, unmanifested souls and unevolved matter. The three aspects of this underworld are interpreted as in the same way: the unconscious aspect is denoted by the left-hand card, the present actuality or physical manifestation by the central one, and the conscious condition by that on the right. Linking the underworldly level with the one above it is the lower linking character, interpreted here as indicating spiritual evolution from a lower state of existence towards manifestation on the material plane. The central triad of characters signifies the present, material world of Middle Earth. This is the realm upon which we exist at the present moment. We interpret these three staves in the same way as those on the underworldly level

Connecting this material world with higher things is the upper linking stave of the cosmic axis. This denotes all of those processes which are tending either to assist or to hinder our spiritual progress towards higher things. Above this linking stave is the upper triad which signifies the higher plane of existence.

This is the heavenly upper world, which is the abode of the divine power and those beings that have evolved above and beyond the earthly plane. We interpret the three staves in this higher level in the same way as those on the other two levels. The only difference is that the central card represents spiritual, rather than material, existence.

The cosmic axis spread is useful because it gives us the two linking staves on the cosmic axis which are the keys of the transformation of the past into the present, and the present into the future. If we wish to discover the factors of transvolution, then we can do this shoat for these cards alone. The lower linking card represents the tendencies and influences which have led from the past to the present, and the upper linking card signifies the influences currently leading the condition from its present state towards a future one. This version of the spread is valuable if we wish to investigate our progress or otherwise upon our chosen spiritual pathway. However, because of its sensitive nature, the questioner should only undertake this interpretation if she or he has a real need of this knowledge. If there are any misgivings, as with all divination and magic, it is better not to do it.

31. The archetypes of time, space and number are represented as a goddess in the Indian Pagan tradition. In this image, based on an 18th century Tantric manuscript, the body of the goddess-as-cosmos reflects the Northern European goddesses Frigg and Our Lady, and the primal giant, Ymir.

Chapter 7
Significant Combinations of Gothic Characters

In a Gothic divination, some combinations of characters can be considered to be more significant or powerful than others. In addition to being significant in divinatory shoats, these combinations are efficacious in rune magic as bind-runes, and as Gothic monograms. Some Gothic characters have greater power or effect than others, and because of this, some combinations are more significant than others. The following combinations are the most useful:

Faihu - Feo

When it is paired with Urus - Uraz, the Gothic rune Faihu or the Gothic stave Feo indicates that the querent is undergoing a process of healing. When it comes up in a reading alongside the rune Ansus or the letter Aza, it denotes - the presence of wealth or success gained through the application of the intellect, and when it is combined with Saúil or Sugil, it denotes wealth through hard work, and with Teiws or Tyz, it indicates power and success. With Othal and Utal, it denotes reward through perseverance and with Dags and Daz, Faihu - Feo specifies increases in wealth. When Faihu - Feo appears in an upright orientation, but with Haal or Hagl inverted, then this array signifies failure.

Urus - Uraz

Urus or Uraz combined with Faihu - Feo indicates the process of effective healing, whilst with Ansus and Aza, it denotes magical powers in operation. With the rune Raida or the stave Reda, Urus and Uraz indicate to the querent that an immediate change is necessary and that he or she has the strength to carry the change through with success. But when Uruz or Uraz are inverted with the rune Raida or the character Reda upright, this indicates that although a change is necessary, the querent lacks the strength to undertake it successfully. Urus or Uraz, inverted with Giba or Gewa or inverted Winja or Winne indicates that the querent is being dominated by a stronger personality than him- or herself. When inverted Urus and Uraz with Egeis - Eyz and Lagus - Laaz indicate that an opportunity is presenting itself which nevertheless ought to be allowed to pass by without being taken up.

Thauris - Thyth

When it occurs alongside the Gothic runes and characters Ansus - Aza, Jer - Gaar and Mannaz - Manna, the rune Thauris and the letter Thyth tells the questioner that she or he should attempt nothing on his or her own at present. With Hagl and Haal, Eis - Iiz or Nauths and Noics, Thauris or Thyth warn us that it is unwise for us to try to proceed with our current projects at present or to attempt anything new at all until later, when the time is right. But with Aihs or Waer and Algs - Ezec, it indicates that a condition of protective good luck is present in the questioner's life. When Thauris or Thyth appears reversed with Raida - Reda, this denotes the querent's control of his or her will, whilst with Kusma and Chosma inverted also, it indicates that the querent has been overtaken or surpassed by a colleague or pupil.

Ansus - Aza

When this character appears upright with Faihu and Feo, it indicates wealth gained through intellectual prowess. Paired with Urus - Uraz, Ansus - Aza indicates that the querent possesses magical abilities, which she or he should learn to utilise properly. Appearing alongside the Gothic characters Winja - Winne, Ansus - Aza denotes creative mental effort. When it is paired with Giba - Gewa, the runic form produces the bind-rune called *Gibu Auja*, which means 'good luck' and brings it. This combination is the best omen for good luck in Gothic divination. When it appears with Jer or Gaar, Ansus and Aza warn the querent that he or she ought to take legal advice on the matter in hand. And when it occurs with Pairthra and Pertra, it indicates that the questioner has to potential to make some rediscovery of hidden knowledge. If it comes up inverted with Pairthra - Pertra also inverted, this stave denotes forgetfulness and the loss of knowledge. With Egeis and Eyz, it indicates a journey. Ansus - Aza with Baírkana or Bercna denote matters concerning the relationship between the parent and his or her child. It may refer to a visit from a parent. With Mannaz - Manna and Lagus or Laaz, which in this context are *hogrunes*, those characters concerned with the mind and consciousness, Ansus - Aza is very significant. With Mannaz or Manna, the combination signifies wisdom, whilst with Lagus or Laaz, academic prowess. Ansus and Aza combined with Baírkana or Bercna in its reversed position signifies some concern about a child.

Raida - Reda

Raida - Reda combined with the rune Kusma or the Gothic stave Chosma indicate that creative work is being undertaken, whilst along with Egeis or Eyz, the characters indicate a journey. With Teiws or Tyz, Raida or Reda promises that any legal litigation in hand will prove successful for the querent. But this is with the important proviso that he or she is in the right. Raida or Reda appearing together with Egeis or Eyz indicate movement, travel and change. If Raida or Reda appear with Pairthra or Pertra in their reversed positions, then this indicates that a promise has been broken. With Algs and Ezec reversed, Raida or Reda denote that the questioner has been deceived or swindled. But when it appears along with an inverted Thauris rune or letter Thyth, then Raida or Reda indicates that the questioner has his or her will under complete control.

Kusma - Chosma

When it appears upright, Kusma and Chosma with Ba"rkana or Bercna or Iggws and Enguz denotes a physical birth. Appearing with Ansus - Aza, Raida - Reda, Winja or Winne, Hagl - Haal or Algs or Ezec, it indicates the accomplishment of creative work. Kusma and Chosma with Saúil - Sugil denotes the power of illumination, seeing clearly.

When they are inverted, Kusma or Chosma with Thauris and Thyth also reversed signifies that one has been overtaken or surpassed by a colleague or pupil. Kusma and Chosma with Nauths - Noics or Eis - Iiz represent delays and a negation of the outgoing nature of the rune. With inverted Nauths and Noics, reversed Kusma or Chosma indicates that the querent is attempting to hold on to a futile relationship, and with reversed Othal - Utal, a binding of one's activities is indicated.

Giba - Gewa

Appearing alongside Ansus, the runic letter Giba creates the bind-rune known as *Gibu Auja*, so this is a particularly auspicious diad. Also, with Winja or Winne, the meaning of the combination is 'gift of joy'. As a bind-rune, this is the symbol utilised by practitioners of the Christian tradition as the *Chi-Rho*, the monogram of the Christ. With Baírkana or Bercna inverted, Giba and Gewa denotes concern over one's partner's health.

Winja - Winne

When it appears in a shoat alongside Ansus - Aza, this character signifies the application of creative mental effort. Paired with Kusma or Chosma, Winja and Winne denotes the performance or results of creative work. With Giba and Gewa, this is the 'gift of joy'. When it appears reversed with binding runes like Nauths - Noics and Eis - Iiz, the prognosis is one of impending misery.

Hagl - Haal

If they come down together in a divination, Hagl - Haal and Raida - Reda signify that any ill-wishes that others have towards the querent will be sent back to their point of origin. With Kusma or Chosma, the rune Hagl and the Gothic letter Haal denote fertility both of mind and body. This may indicate a possible physical birth, or alternatively the accomplishment of creative work. With Nauths - Noics, Hagl and Haal denote the imminence of an unexpected event which is likely to be to the question-maker's detriment.

When Hagl - Haal comes down with Eis or Iiz or Othal - Utal inverted, delay is to be expected, perhaps in the form of an interruption of our projects. With Jer or Gaar, this rune and letter indicate that the querent is trying with little success to pursue a career or a way of life for which he or she is not suited. Paired with Pairthra or Pertra, it denotes that the

32. The character Winja - Winne takes the form of the wind-vanes formerly used on sailing ships in the Baltic and North Sea traditions. This drawing depicts one that still exists at the church of Heggen in Norway.

querent may expect to gain money by a means other than work. Teiws and Tyz and Hagl - Haal interact to bring into play our creative, formative, abilities. Hagl - Haal and Dags - Daz indicate that the querent expects failure, and is thus behaving in negative ways that cannot bring success. Paired with inverted characters and runes, Hagl or Haal denotes transformation which emphasises the negative qualities that the reversed runes represent. Similarly, inverted Hagl and Haal coming down on the shoat alongside upright staves has the same meaning.

Nauths - Noics

When the Gothic rune Nauths and the Gothic letter Noics appears alongside another rune or stave, it effects a binding that acts upon that other character's meaning. When it appears in a shoat along with success-oriented figures including Faihu and Feo, Ansus or Aza and Saúil - Sugil, it warns us that we ought not to make previously-planned alterations in our life. When Nauths - Noics appears with Hagl - Haal, this combination indicates that it is likely that a sudden, impersonal, delaying event will occur. This combination can also denote that an incoming attack or harmful event will be blocked. When Nauths - Noics appears with Jer or Gaar, this denotes that the questioner will be compelled to make recompense for a mistake or offence committed in the past. When it is inverted, the Gothic rune Nauths and the letter Noics also indicate delay and binding.

Eis - Iiz

It is a general principle of this Gothic character that Eis - Iiz puts a static binding or operational brake upon the signification of the characters with which it is appears in a divination. With Hagl and Haal, Nauths - Noics indicates that

the querent's progress will be slowed or stopped. There is an indication that projects will be hindered or brought to a halt. When combined with Dags, the rune Eis creates the sigil of the Labrys, the double-axe which is the emblem of the Great Goddess, and also, as in the case of the axe of the founder of the Kingdom of the Isle of Man, King Orry, a symbol of irresistible authority. When it comes down in a divination alongside Thauris - Thyth or Nauths - Noics reversed, the stave Eis - Iiz indicates that there may well be considerable frustration and delay to the querent.

Jer - Gaar

When in a shoat, the Gothic rune Jer or the Gothic letter Gaar come down with Ansus or Aza, the combination tells the querent that he or she ought to take legal advice with regard to the matter in question. Combined with Nauths or Noics, it warns us that recompense must be made for mistakes we have made in the past. When Jer or Gaar is paired with Pairthra - Pertra, this array denotes the possibility of the inquirer profiting from an inheritance. Jer - Gaar upright alongside Mannaz or Manna in the inverted position indicate the likelihood of a legal wrangle, whilst with the rune Sa'il or the stave Sugil, Jer and Gaar indicate recovery from illness.

Aihs - Waer

When this rune-character appears with Thauris or Thyth in the upright orientation, this array denotes protection against harm. When it is aligned with Sa'il or Sugil and Algs - Ezec, the Gothic rune Aihs and the character Waer denotes that magical protection is present against all ills. It is a general principle that when the staves Aihs and Waer come down reversed in a shoat, this denotes defeat and failure. Aihs and Waer combined with Raida - Reda indicates that the inquirer

has been tricked by someone else. Perhaps this will result in severe losses for the questor. When Waer appears inverted with Quairtra also reversed, then the querent's prospects are very bad indeed.

Pairthra - Pertra

This Gothic stave is associated with sexuality, and when the questor asks an appropriate question, Pairthra - Pertra with the upright forms of Urus - Uraz, Kusma or Chosma, Giba - Gewa, Teiws or Tyz, Bairkana - Bercna or Lagus - Laaz indicates sexual compatibility. But if these staves, or the Pairthra - Pertra stone or card appear in an inverted orientation, then there are serious problems of compatibility.

When Pairthra and Pertra appear along with Faihu - Feo or Hagl - Haal, this promises the inquirer the prospect of a sudden gain of money. This is usually unearned money, such as one might receive for a winning bet on the horses or a fortunate lottery ticket. If Paitrhta - Pertra appears with Jer or Gaar and Othal or Utal, then this indicates monetary gain from a legacy or inheritance.

Algs - Ezec

A shoat where Algs - Ezec appears with Thauris - Thyth in their upright positions indicates to us that we are protected from all harmful influences. With Aihs - Waer, we obtain the same meaning, but this time with a more magical connotation. When Algs or Ezec come down with Saúil or Sugil, this indicates that the inquirer is shielded from her or his immediate problems.

33. Ulli, god of winter, skiing and hunting with bow and arrow.
Seventeenth-century Swedish engraving.

Saúil - Sugil

The bright solar properties of Saúil and Sugil improve the meaning of any runes with which they may come down in a shoat. However, there may be problems because of the amount of power that Saúil - Sugil brings. Rather than slowing down, binding or negating the querent's prospects, these staves may overemphasise and overaccelerate events, which is sometimes as undesirable as the negativity that we usually consider to be harmful. When Saúil or Sugil appear in a shoat with Raida - Reda or Winja - Winne, they indicate that the inquirer is incapable of slowing down his or her progress, usually meaning that he or she is obsessed with work to the detriment of almost everything else in life.

This out-of-control power is expressed most powerfully when Sauil or Sugil comes down with Kusma - Chosma and Teiws - Tyz. Respectively, these combinations emphasise the enlightenment and energy of the individual. When these solar characters appear combined with Algs - Ezec, they signify the power of being shielded, denoting protection against all harmful influences that might be abroad.

When they appear in a shoat along with Giba - Gewa, Iggws - Enguz and Dags or Daz, the solar staves Saúil and Sugil signify that balance will be restored, and that appropriate conditions for health are appearing. This includes recovery from depression. When the question refers to illness or disease, combined with Jer or Gaar and Mannaz or Manna, the solar staves denote a rapid recovery. When they are paired with binding runes such as Nauths and Noics, Eis and Iiz, Hagl - Haal, and Thauris or Thyth in their reversed stance, although the effect of these runes is still present, it is considerably minimised by the solar strength. When Saúil and Sugil appear alongside Aihs or Waer, this indicates that the inquirer is shielded from his or her problems.

Teiws - Tyz

To the Goths, the god represented by this character was probably the most respected deity. Known by many names, from his ancient name of Tîwaz, the Anglo-Saxon Tiw, his Norse version Tyr, and, from the East Anglian Nameless Art, Termagant, this god was said to be the same as the Roman god Mars. His Gothic rune and letter is therefore one of great power. Consequently, when it appears in a shoat upright Teiws - Tyz in general will tend to reinforce the beneficial, powerful, aspects of any character with which it is paired. Thus, when it comes up with the Gothic rune Faihu or the Gothic character Feo, the Termagant stave Teiws or Tyz indicates awesome power and financial success. When it appears alongside the staves Raida or Reda, this combination denotes success in legal matters.

Of course, as the Great God Termagant is deity of right orderliness, this will be successful only providing the querent's case is just. When the Teiws - Tyz character appears with Winja or Winne, it indicates lasting joy for the questor. When Hagl - Haal appears with Teiws - Tyz, this combination indicates the presence of creative, formative, powers. With Aihs and Waer, the Termagant stave denotes the presence of the personal magical power of Megin. If it appears in a shoat alongside the Gothic rune Pairthra or the stave Pertra, Teiws - Tyz denotes the operation of sexual attraction, and when it is paired with the solar power of Saúil and Sugil, the Termagant-rune denotes real power and physical success. But when it appears paired with Mannaz and Manna in their inverted orientation, this indicates that the querent will be involved in some kind of fight.

However, this will result in a successful outcome for the inquirer. With Mannaz or Manna inverted, Teiws or Tyz in its inverted orientation indicates a fight which will be lost, and when the querent is female, the Termagant rune appearing upright along with Lagus or Laaz specifies that she must undertake a struggle to assert her rights. When the rune Teiws or the stave Tyz appears in its reversed orientation alongside the Mother Earth characters Othal and Utal, it may indicate the liability that the inquirer may suffer an accident or accidents.

Bairkana - Bercna

When the goddess-oriented character Bairkana - Bercna comes down in a shoat along with Ansus - Aza, this indicates that the parent - child relationship is relevant to the questor's inquiry. Sometimes, this combination indicates a visit from a close relative. When the Gothic rune Baírkana or the Gothic character Bercna appears in a divination reversed alongside Ansus or Aza upright, this combination indicates that the querent has some anxiety about a child. When the Birch rune appears in its inverted orientation alongside Giba or Gewa, it indicates some concern over the health of the inquirer's partner. But when Baírkana or Bercna appears with Mannaz or Manna this combination tells us that it is unwise for us to make a decision at the present.

Egeis - Eyz

When it appears in a shoat upright with Raida and Reda, the Gothic rune Egeis or the Gothic letter Eyz denotes a journey. Appearing alongside with Kusma or Chosma, Egeis or Eyz represents the questor's ego under full control of the will, and with Mannaz - Manna, this is reinforced, for this is the assertive statement, "I am". Together in a shoat, Egeis - Eyz and Lagus - Laaz signify confusion and dissolution, whilst together, Iggws - Enguz and Egeis - Eyz promise longevity. When it appears in its inverted form along with Urus - Uraz, the stave Egeis - Eyz points to a change of plans, or warns of an unexpected event. When it is reversed with the staves Raida and Reda or Lagus - Laaz, this combination indicates a long, one-way journey, perhaps a removal from one's home or even emigration from one's homeland.

Mannaz - Manna

Mannaz - Manna appearing in the divination reading along with Ansus - Aza brings the powerful support of the *Hogrunes,* the characters of knowledge and wisdom. Combinations of the Gothic staves Mannaz - Manna with Othal - Utal in their inverted form or Eis - Iiz, Thauris or Thyth, Nauths - Noics and Ba"rkana or Bercna upright, warn the questor that he or she would do well to postpone any important decisions until a later time. When Mannaz or Manna appears in a shoat along with Lagus or Laaz, the reading indicates intellectual strength. But when it is inverted, the Gothic rune Mannaz and the Gothic character Manna will tend to cancel or counteract the influence of any other rune or character with which it appears. Combined with the stave Jer - Gaar, Mannaz - Manna warns of the potential that the querent will become involved in a legal argument. When it appears with Teiws or Tyz in its upright position, this indicates an all-out fight. If the Termagant rune is inverted, then the fight is likely to be lost.

Lagus - Laaz

A shoat that has Lagus - Laaz upright with Ansus - Aza tells the querent that academic success is in the offing. When this watery symbol appears in a divination alongside an upright Egeis or Eyz, this combination warns of confusion and rapid dissolution of the present state of things, as it does with Dags and Daz, whilst with Egeis and Eyz inverted, Lagus - Laaz denotes a long, one-way journey, perhaps emigration from one's homeland.

144

When Lagus - Laaz and Mannaz - Manna appear together, this indicates that the querent is applying his or her proper intellectual strength to the matter in question. Appearing in a shoat with the Termagant rune Teiws or Tyz, Lagus or Laaz indicates a fight for the rights of women. Lagus - Laaz combined with Ing reversed is a sign of distress and sorrow, and when it appears reversed with Jer or Gaar, it indicates that the inquirer's minor transgressions will be exposed to public view.

Iggws - Enguz

When Iggws or Enguz appears along with another Gothic rune or character, it emphasises any qualities of transition or completion that the character may express. When it appears combined with Egeis - Eyz, Iggws - Enguz signifies longevity, whilst inverted with Lagus - Laaz, it denotes grief and distress.

Othal or Utal

When it appears in a reading upright alongside the staves Ansus - Aza or Mannaz - Manna, the Gothic rune Othal or the character Utal denotes a visionary ideal in the mind. This is a perfect expression of the will in action, the essence of true magic. When it is paired with Faihu or Feo, Jer - Gaar or Baírkana - Bercna, the Othal and Utal staves signify meanness, miserliness and materialism. When they appear with Urus - Uraz and Pairthra - Pertra, this stave tells us that the if she or he perseveres, the questor is likely to succeed., Othal - Utal coming down the shoat with Dags - Daz signifies that an increase in the questor's prestige is imminent. Combined with an inverted Termagant rune, Othal - Utal tells us that the inquirer is likely to suffer an accident. A reversed

34. In the Northern Tradition, the Bard is the visionary who puts into poetry and song thosae aspects of human existence and experience that can never be expressed in any other way. Seated on the tartan Web of Wyrd, he plays the divine harmony on his harp.

Othal or Utal character paired with Hagl - Haal denotes delay and interruption of current processes. Appearing alongside Mannaz and Manna, this stave exhorts the questioner to delay making any imminent decisions, whilst with Dags or Daz, it warns the subject that he or she is thinking pessimistically at present.

Dags - Daz

When it appears in a divination with the Audhumla-staves Faíhu - Feo, Dags - Daz promises the querent an increase in wealth, and when it is seen with Baírkana or Bercna and Lagus - Laaz, the growing, expansive, qualities denoted by these staves are empowered and enhanced. But when it comes down the shoat with Thauris or Thyth, Dags or Daz warns that there is some intransigence about. Also, when the Dags - Daz falls together with Not or Is, it minimises their negative, binding, qualities. With Eis - Iiz the figure of the Labrys so created can well indicate the presence or effects of inflexible, authoritarian, behaviour. When Dags or Daz occurs with Lagus or Laaz, the combination signifies confusion. Dags - Daz combined with Othal or Utal indicate that for the querent there is some increase in prestige. If Dags - Daz comes down in a shoat combination with Winja or Winne or equally with Mannaz - Manna in their inverted position, then this must be taken as a warning that the questor is thinking negatively. When potentially bad or negatively-inverted staves appear paired with Dags or Daz, they are mitigated into a far less dangerous form.

Quairtra

As the quintessence, the Gothic letter Quairtra tends to emphasise the qualities of any other rune or stave. It intensifies the effect of their pure essence just as a fire burns away the dross surrounding the pure metal. Thus, Quairtra in itself is neither good nor bad, all positive or negative readings in a divination coming from the stave within which Quairtra is paired.

Triads of Characters

In addition to significant dyads of staves, there are also a number of powerful combinations which involve three characters. Threes appear in many of the important spreads which are used in Gothic divination, such as the Cosmic Axis and the Grid of Nine. Unlike with the combinations above where either may come first, the order of characters in triadic arrays are significant. When we read them from left to right, according to European alphabetic tradition, certain triads create words that are significant in the Northern Tradition. Occasionally, this more literal, or literary, meaning may override the esoteric meaning of the combined characters. But, because European magical alphabets come from inspired sources, it is more usual that the kennings and the stave-interpretation of the words thus created are in perfect agreement with one another. Unless noted otherwise, the characters referred to here must appear in their upright orientation.

The characters Ansus - Aza, Lagus or Laaz and Urus or Uraz make up the magical word Alu, which, in rune magic, signifies ale, which esoterically is the empowering 'water of life', or, in bardic terms, the fluid that carries of the primal power of the goddesses and gods. This triad is a powerful combination of staves that bodes well, promising good things, and changes for the better. The word Alu denotes the qualities of ecstacy, with the recipient being under divine guardianship. In a divination, this triad's appearance shows that these desirable qualities are working for the questioner's benefit. When the triad of Ansus - Aza, Faihu - Feo and Iggws - Enguz appear, they denote the querent's release from a problematic situation, suggesting that all of the things that are binding up or hindering his or her life will soon be broken through or passed by. Together, Ansus - Aza, Winja or Winne and Othal - Utal denote the triadic aspects of the godly Allfather, manifested as the deities Odin, Vili and Vé, or in the Trinitarian sect of Christianity, the Father, Son and Holy Ghost. When this triad appears in a shoat, it indicates that the questioner will be able to attain perfect harmony of her or his life with her or his true will, so long as the querent continues to pursue his or her chosen path.

The Gothic staves Ansus or Aza, Saúil - Sugil and Kusma or Chosma combine to produce the Northern Tradition magical word Asc, the Ash-tree. This refers to Yggdrassil, the sacred world-ash-tree of the gods in Norse mythology. In a shoat, this triad tells us that we possess the power to survive any attacks that are being made on us at present, and that we will come unscathed through adversity. When Winja or Winne, Othal - Utal and Dags or Daz are combined in a divination, they make the word Wod, a wrd meaning divine frenzy, as in the name of the god Woden (a version of the name Odin). This triad appearing in a reading denotes the joyful transformation of a seemingly-bad situation through inspired action.

When the staves Urus or Uraz, Lagus - Laaz and Faihu - Feo are combined in a divination, they form the magical word Ulf. This is another power-word, signifying the awesome and almost irresistible power of the wolf. In a divination, this triad tells us that there is a powerful force assisting us. The Gothic bishop Ulfilas, and many warriors from the Northern Tradition martial arts bore the name and thus the magical virtues of the wolf. The three Gothic staves Jer - Gaar, Raida or Reda and Thauris - Thyth, when combined, form the runic power-word Jrᚦ, which is Jörth, the Earth. When this triad appears in a shoat, it denotes the return of appropriate conditions that have been absent for a while. But success will result only if the querent is willing and able to work in harmony with 'the way of the world'.

Generally, triadic combinations in the shoat of the early winter runes Hagl - Haal, Eis - Iiz and Nauths - Noics signify delay and binding. This specific combination Hagl - Haal, Eis - Iiz and Nauths - Noics make the word Hin. This triad tell us that we are experiencing a distancing and a hindering of things from their due course. Hin brings us delays and hindrances, severely restricting our actions. This may appear in the form of illness - Old Hin is the East Anglian demon who is believed to cause the illness known as influenza. Similarly, Nauths or Noics, along with Eis - Iiz and Lagus - Laaz makes a triad of negation, producing the epitome of nothingness, the word Nil. In a shoat, this triad presages the total destruction or obliteration of the matter in question, if the querent does not take immediate drastic measures to avert disaster. The following two triads of Dags or Daz, Raida - Reda inverted and Lagus or Laaz, or alternatively Dags - Daz, Egeis or Eyz and Lagus - Laaz warn us that confusion and disruption may come to our cherished projects. When these triads appear, then it is timely that we to delay any important decisions and re-appraise the situation before acting. Another negative divination is one that brings us the characters Thauris - Thyth reversed, Eis - Iizs and Nauths or Noics, gives us a reading that shows that an irresistible force of binding and delay is acting upon the querent. There is only one possibility when such an indication appears in a shoat; the querent must abandon the project or circumstance in question, and change course at once.

Completely different from the foregoing triads is the array of Kusma or Chosma, Dags - Daz and Saúil or Sugil. Together, these three signify brilliant illumination. This illumination is working on every level, from the inner illumination of the unconscious, through the brightness of high day in the physical world, to the brilliant light of the Sun illuminating the conscious mind. This is a Gothic character-triad of powerful enlightenment, giving the querent a completely new and powerful approach to problem-solving. When the come down together on the casting cloth, the Gothic characters Giba or Gewa, Ansus - Aza and Raida - Reda combine to make the word Gar, the name of the irresistible magic spear of Odin. The kenning of this ash-shafted magical weapon demonstrates a beneficial power that soon will come to the assistance of the querent. The three staves Egeis - Eyz, Ansus - Aza and Mannaz - Manna together in a reading denote that through the application of our knowledge to the question, we will have a fortunate outcome that shows wise judgement to have been used. Egeis or Eyz, Iggws - Enguz and Ansus - Aza together indicate that there soon will come a closer communion between the querent and the more esoteric secrets of life.

The triad of Giba or Gewa, Iggws or Enguz and Egeis - Eyz give the querent the message that the matter in question will not be solved readily, but may drag out for a long time. All he or she can do is to endure it with patience and fortitude. The triad of Giba - Gewa, Mannaz or Manna and Winja or Winne, however, indicate that soon there will be a reconciliation, the healing of rifts and disagreements between individuals, promising a more harmonious future together. When the Gothic letters Gewa, Pairthra and Winne appear together in a shoat, they represent the querent's attainment of stable, unselfish contentment. Jer - Gaar, Urus or Uraz and Saúil or Sugil together indicate that the process of healing of the illness, or solution of the problem, is taking place, however unapparent that may be at present.

When the three Gothic staves called Jer or Gaar, Faihu - Feo and Winja or Winne appear in the shoat with one another, they signify the bringing-together of all of those things that provide us with an abundant, joyful, life. Together, the staves Algs - Ezec, Othal or Utal and Thauris - Thyth tell us that some powerful protection is available. This triad informs us that we are correct in taking the action in question, and that fortunately we are defended, whether we know it or not, against any bad consequences which might result from our actions. The triad containing Pairthra - Pertra, Ansus - Aza

**Iouis siue Panos Hierogly-
phica repræsentatio.**

A Facies rubicunda, caloris vis in Mundo.
B Radiorum cœlestium in sublunaria vir-
C Elementa masculina.   (tus.
D Potestas in annû omnesq; reuolutiones.
E Virtote eius omnia fulciuntur.
F Dominium in firmamentûm , seu fixa-
    rum stellarum sphæriæ.
G Terra (elementum fœmin.) hispida
    plantis, satis, arboribusque.
H Aquæ & liquoris fons (elem. fœm.) ri-
    gatione fœcundans terram.
I Agri, segetes, aliaque vegetabilia .
K Harmonia 7. Planetarum.
L Aspera & inæqualia montes indicant.
M Vis fœcunditaria.
N Stabile fundamentum.
O Vis ventorum, & celeritas in agendo.

35. The Great God Pan, god of Nature whose image denotes his equal
presence in the mineral, plant, animal, human and divine realms.

and Raida or Reda indicate that hidden or forgotten knowledge will be recovered. When the shoat gives us this reading, we must recognise that this is telling us to undertake further enquiries into the matter in hand, as it is likely that we have failed to recognise some important factor. Together, Pairthra - Pertra, Ansus - Aza and Nauths - Noics indicate that the questor needs to bring himself or herself into harmony with the necessary processes of existence, or failure will result. These three runes make the name of the Great God Pan, deity of Nature and the link between our lower and higher selves, if we look at it in that way.

As with the Great God Pan, other triads can come together to make the names of gods and goddesses. For instance, the triad made of Saúil or Sugil, Othal - Utal and Lagus or Laaz makes the name of the solar goddess Sol, which, of course, indicates the brilliant nurturing and creative energies of the Sun. When this triad appears in a shoat, it tells us that we have the strength and stability to cope well enough with any changes which may appear to be be imminent. Similarly, Saúil - Sugil, Teiws - Tyz and Raida or Reda together indicate that the inquirer will have a very successful outcome in any conflicts which may arise soon, especially in justified legal actions. Another deity triad arises when the staves Baírkana or Bercna, Ansus or Aza and Raida - Reda are combined to make the word Bar. In rune-magic, this denotes the bear, or, more precisely the power of a show of strength as the best means of defence. When this triad appears in a shoat, it is interpreted as meaning that the inquirer may have the ability to bluff his or her way through a confrontation by an outer show of strength without ever having to use force, either physical or legal. Bar informs us to stand firm and to resist all external pressures that might descend upon us.

The three Gothic runes and characters Othal - Utal, Not and Dags or Daz combine to form the runic word ÖND, This denotes the vital breath or universal soul of all things. The triad thus signifies the questioner's conquest of seemingly insuperable problems by aligning her- or himself with the necessity of the circumstances, and by so doing, transcending them. Similarly, the characters Othal or Utal, Thauris - Thyth and Raida or Reda coming together make the name of Othr, a quality or archetype personified in Norse tradition as one of the consorts of the goddess Freyja. In a reading, this triad denotes the delicate balance that must always be maintained between stability and motion. It is this balance that we must consider when we choose to explore other areas outside those which are accepted as 'normal' or 'conventional'.

APPENDIX 1
The Basic Meanings of the Gothic Staves

The meanings listed here are a contemporary interpretation of the meanings of the Gothic runes and Gothic alphabetic letters. They have been used by the author for many years in divination, and have proved to be meaningful and effective. Questions concerning the historical usage of these meanings are quite a different issue from their contemporary use.

The works of Otto von Friesen and Sigurd Agrell, for instance, give certain insights into the mentality of the ancient users. All things that exist in the present must develop or die, and it is the same with systems of divination.

If we attempt to ignore örlog, and pretend that nothing has happened over the last 1000 or so years, then we must operate within a fictitious framework, and the Gothic divination system will only be valid as an adjunct to this fantasy world. However, if we apply this ancient oracular and magical system to the world as it exists, then we will find it of immediate use to-day.

The contemporary meanings are in the following list:

36. Mider, Manx guardian of the underworld, whose gate is guarded by the three cranes.

Rune - Gothic Letter	Meanings and Correspondences
Faihu - Fe:	cattle, wealth, abundance.
Urus - Uraz:	the Aurochs, primal strength, perseverance.
Thauris - Thyth:	thorn, giant-power, the Crystal Sphere, protection.
Ansus - Aza:	the God-power, speech, intellectual power, poetic abilities.
Raida - Reda:	riding, wheel, motion, the vehicle, ritual process, creative power.
Kusma - Chosma:	pine torch, light in the darkness, a wound, spiritual illumination.
Giba - Gewa:	gift of the gods, talent/burden.
Winja - Winne:	joy, contentment, prosperity, movement in harmony with conditions.
Hagl - Haal: hail,	formative causation, underlying structures.
Nauths - Noics:	need, necessity, binding, an old woman.
Eis - Iiz:	ice, cessation, static power, inexorable processes.
Jer - Gaar:	season, completion, fruitfulness, return.
Aihs - Waer:	yew tree, bow and arrow, physical and magical defence, sacrifice, the mysteries of life and death.
Pairthra - Pertra:	the pot, the womb, the solar halo.
Algs - Ezec:	elk, defensive strength, resistance, the Fifteen Stars.
Saúil - Sugil:	the Sun, brightness, energy, success through magical willpower.
Teiws - Tyz:	the God Tᴕwaz-Mars, the sword, power, male sexuality, victory and achievement.
Baírkana - Bercna:	The Great Mother Goddess, birch tree, fecundity, purification, the power of the bear.
Egeis - Eyz:	horse, motion, transformation,

	partnership, the cosmic breath, Ùnd.
Mannaz - Manna:	human being, the tree, mediator between the heavens and the Earth.
Lagus - Laaz:	water, flow, life-energy, Moon-power, the subconscious mind.
Iggws - Enguz:	the God Ingv— and the goddess Yngona, fire, fertility, limitless expansion and protection, a doorway to the astral.
Othal - Utal:	Mother Earth, homestead, enclosure, ancestral property, possession.
Dags - Daz:	day, the light of high noon, invisibility, entry, sudden changes.
Quairtra:	Cosmic fire, the Quintessence, the encapsulation of the all in the one.

APPENDIX 2
The Houses or Sectors of the 24 Characters

In runic astrology and location-work, the 24 Houses or Sectors are defined geometrically. Each House occupies a sector that occupies one twenty-fourth of the circumference, a portion measuring 15 degrees of arc. Each of the directions called an aetting defines the central-point of a sector, which means that the 24-piece circle commences at one forty-eighth part of a circle westward of due south (7° 30' west of south). For further details of the techniques of the runic time cycles, see my *Runic Astrology* (Capall Bann, 1995).

If we view this circle in terms of the sun-dial, the Gothic characters correspond with the following hours:

Faihu - Fe	12.30 - 13.30.
Urus - Uraz	13.30 - 14.30.
Thauris - Thyth	14.30 - 15.30.
Ansus - Aza	15.30 - 16.30.
Raida - Reda	16.30 - 17.30.
Kusma - Chosma	17.30 - 18.30.
Giba - Gewa	18.30 - 19.30.
Winja - Winne	19.30 - 20.30.
Hagl - Haal	20.30 - 21.30.
Nauths - Noics	21.30 - 22.30.
Eis - Iiz	22.30 - 23.30.
Jer - Gaar	23.30 - 00.30.

Aihs - Waer	00.30 - 01.30.
Pairthra - Pertra	01.30 - 02.30.
Algs - Ezec	02.30 - 03.30.
Saúil - Sugil	03.30 - 04.30.
Tiews - Tyz	04.30 - 05.30.
Baírkana - Bercna	05.30 - 06.30.
Egeis - Eyz	06.30 - 07.30.
Mannaz - Manna	07.30 - 08.30.
Lagus - Laaz	08.30 - 09.30.
Iggws - Enguz	09.30 - 10.30.
Othal - Utal	10.30 - 11.30.
Dags - Daz	11.30 - 12.30.

The Gothic stave Quairtra is not part of the day- and year-circle. When it is used, it signifies microcosmically the unchanging central point around which the year rotates, and macrocosmically the entire circle.

APPENDIX 3
Annual Time-Correspondences of the Gothic Runes and Characters

Below are the Gregorian calendar dates on which commences the ruling power of each character in the corresponding half-month. In divination, the dates can be used for determining the significator in stone or card readings. Times are given for Local Apparent Time, that is, the actual time measured by the relative position of the sun, not according to local time zones which reflect the needs of commerce and politics, ignoring the magical qualities of each period of real time. Times in this table are 'rounded off' to the nearest whole hour, which is about as accurate as it is reasonable to expect. Times at these cusps between the half-months are mutable, and may show the influence of the preceding or following quality, or some combination of them.

Faihu - Fe: 3.00 June 29 until 8.00 July 14.
Urus - Uraz: 8.00 July 14 until 14.00 July 29.
Thauris - Thyth: 14.00 July 29 until 19.00 August 13.
Ansus - Aza: 19.00 August 13 until 0.00 August 29.
Raida - Reda   0.00 August 29 until 6.00 September 13.
Kusma - Chosma   6.00 September 13 until 11.00 September 28.
Giba - Gewa   11.00 September 28 until 16.00 October 13.
Winja - Winne   16.00 October 13 until 22.00 October 28.
Hagl - Haal   22.00 October 28 until 3.00 November 13.
Nauths - Noics: 3.00 November 13 until 8.00 November 28.
Eis - Iiz   8.00 November 28 until 14.00 December 13.

37. The runestaff is the key to the wheel of the months. Engraving from the works of Olaus Magnus.

Jer - Gaar:	14.00 December 13 until 19.00 December 28.
Aihs - Waer	19.00 December 28 until 1.00 January 13.
Pairthra - Pertra	1.00 January 13 until 5.00 January 28.
Algs - Ezec:	5.00 January 28 until 10.00 February 12.
Saúil - Sugil:	10.00 February 12 until 16.00 February 27.
Teiws - Tyz	16.00 February 27 until 21.00 March 14.
Baírkana - Bercna	21.00 March 14 until 2.00 March 30.
Egeis - Eyz	2.00 March 30 until 7.00 April 14.
Mannaz - Manna:	7.00 April 14 until 12.00 April 29.
Lagus - Laaz	12.00 April 29 until 18.00 May 14.
Iggws - Enguz	18.00 May 14 until 23.00 May 29.
Othal - Utal:	23.00 May 29 until 4.00 June 14.
Dags - Daz	4.00 June 14 until 3.00 June 29.
Quairtra	ever present.

APPENDIX 4
Correspondences of the Gothic Runes and Characters

Listed below is a selection magical correspondences of each character aligned with its appropriate tree, herb, polarity, element and Pagan deity. They are not the only possible correspondences, but they are those which the author has found most appropriate and useful within the Gothic context. They can be used in the interpretation of divinations, in magical workings and in contemplative or meditational practices.

Character Name	tree	polarity	element	goddess/god/being.
Faihu - Fe:	elder	male	fire/earth	Audhumla, Frey, Freyja, Abundantia.
Urus - Uraz:	birch	male	earth	Thor, Jupiter, Urd, Clotho.
Thauris - Thyth	oak/thorn	male	fire	Thor, Thrud, Jupiter, Trolls.
Ansus - Aza:	ash	male	air	Odin, the Aesir, God The Father.
Raida - Reda	oak	female	air	Ingvé, Nerthus, Verdandi, Lachesis, Ré, Emania.
Kusma - Chosma	pine	male	fire	Odin, Freyja, Snotra, Var, Vür.
Giba - Gewa	ash/elm	female	air	Friagabis, Abundantia, Gefn.
Winja - Winne	ash	female	earth	Frigg, the Queen of Elfland.

Rune	Tree	Gender	Element	Deities
Hagl - Haal	yew	neuter	ice	Holda, Hecate, Hela.
Nauths - Noics:	beech/rowan	female	fire	Nott, Nut, Nox, Hecate, Justitia, Skuld, Atropos.
Eis - Iiz	alder	neuter	ice	Rinda, Verdandi, Lachesis.
Jer - Gaar:	oak	neuter	earth	Frey, Freyja, Frigg, Libera, Janus.
Aihs - Waer	yew	male	all	Skadi, Ulli, Vuldr.
Pairthra - Pertra	beech/aspen	female	water	Frigg, Cerridwen, Allmother, Lady Luck, Sól.
Algs - Ezec:	yew/service	male	air	Disir, Juno.
Saúil - Sugil:	juniper/bay	neuter	air	Balder, Bale, Phoebe, Sól, Saule, Sunna, Barbet.
Teiws - Tyz:	oak	male	air	Tơwaz, Mars, Tyr, Termagant, Ziu, Zisa, Juno.
Baírkana - Bercna	birch	female	earth	Percht, Nerthus, Holda, Mordgud.
Egeis - Eyz	oak/ash	male	earth	Frey, Freyja, Odin, Epona.
Mannaz - Manna:	holly	male	air	Rig-Heimdall, Askr, Embla.
Lagus - Laaz	willow	male	water	Luna, Poseidon, Aegir, Ran, Njörd.
Iggws - Enguz	apple	male	water/earth	Ingvé, Yngona, Verdandi, Lachesis.
Othal - Utal:	hawthorn	neuter	earth	Nerthus, Gaea, Tellus Mater, Erda, Fjörgynn.
Dags - Daz	spruce	male	fire/air	Syn, Mordgud, Mider.
Quairtra	yew	neuter	all	Loge, Vulcan, Wayland, Daedalus.

APPENDIX 5
Glossary of names and terms

Aett	One eighth of the horizon, one of the eight compass directions (N), see Airt.
Airt	Point of the compass, direction of the wind, a way (S).
Asgard	The abode of the Gods (N).
Askr	The first man, fashioned from an Ash tree (N).
Atropos	The third of the Greek fates, who destroys (cf. Skuld).
Balder	Norse solar god.
Bragi	God of poetry and eloquence (N).
Calas	Solidity, one of the three states of being in Bardic cosmology (W).
Ceridwen	Welsh goddess of life and death.
Clotho	First Greek fate (= Urd).
Embla	The first woman, fashioned from an Elm tree (N).
Forseti	God of laws, whose sacred island is Heligoland (Fr).
Frey(r)	'The Lord': God of fertility and creativity (N).
Friagabis	The 'free giver' goddess (N).
Gefn	'The Giver' goddess (N).
Heimdall	The watcher-god (N).

Hel :	The goddess of death and the underworld (N).
Ingvé	God of protection and fertility (= Frey, q.v.) (OE).
Irminsul	The sacred Teutonic world-pillar, representing the world-tree, the parallel of Yggdrassil, set up at what is now the town of Ober-Marsberg, Germany (G).
Kenning	Poetic allusion or metaphor (OE).
Kvasir	Magic being whose blood made the mead of inspiration (N).
Lachesis	The second Greek fate (= Verdandi).
Lofn	Goddess of forbidden love (N).
Megin	A personal force, distinct from strength or physical power, the possession of which assures good fortune (N).
Mider	Manx guardian of the gates of the underworld.
Mordgud	Goddess who guards the entrance to the underworld (N).
Njörd	God of seafaring, stiller of fire and the waves (N).
Norns	The three parts of existence, personified as Skuld, Urd and Verdandi (q.v.)(N) = the Weird Sisters (OE), the Parcae (Gr)..
Nwyvre	The universal life-breath or force = önd, prana, ki (W) (cf. Vouivre).
Odin	God of inspiration, poetry and combat (N).
odhr	Inspiration. (N)
önd	The universal life breath or force = Nwyvre (N).
örlog	literally 'primal layers' or 'primal laws': that which makes 'now' (N).

Percht	Goddess of growing things, and guardian of as-yet-unborn souls (G).
Ragnarök	Cataclysmic destruction of the world, followed by a regenerated new age ruled by the god Vidar (q.v.)(N).
Rinda	Goddess of the frozen earth (N).
Rig(r)	By-name of Heimdall (q.v.), legendary organiser of human society (N).
Rune	Character from the ancient Germanic alphabet.
Runic Hour	Hour in the day corresponding to a specific rune.
Shoat	The area over and along which runestones or slivers are thrown in rune-casting (A-S, E).
Skuld	The third Norn, That which is to become = the future (N).
Sliver	A flat slice of wood cut to bear runes for divination or as a talisman (EA).
Termagant	God of strength and continuance (= Mars, q.v. Tyr) (EA).
Thor	Norse god of thunder and agriculture.
Thrud	Daughter of Thor (N).
Tyr	God of self-defence, 'The Valiant' (N).
Urd(a)	The first Norn, That which was = the past.
Var	Goddess who punishes oath-breakers (N).
Verdandi	The second Norn, That which is becoming = the present (N).
Vidar	Son of Odin (q.v.), god of the New Age after Ragnarök (N).
Vouivre	Dragon-like personification of the universal life-breath in the Earth: 'earth energies' (q.v. Nwyvre) (Ga, F).
Völva	a wise woman (N).

Wyrd	One's personal 'fate' or 'destiny', but also generally, 'the way things go'(A-S).
Xoanon	A portable god-image used by the Goths (Gr).
Yngvé-Frey	By-name of Ing (q.v.)(N).
Yggdrassil	Literally 'the horse of Ygg' (a by-name of Odin, q.v.); the cosmic axial world tree of Norse tradition (N).
Yule	The festival of midwinter, now amalgamated with Christmas (E, EA, N, Sc).
Zisa	Swabian goddess-consort of Tyr (q.v.).
Ziu	Swabian god (= Tyr, Termagant).

Abbreviations:
E: English.
EA: East Anglian.
F: French.
Fr: Frisian.
G: German.
Ga: Gaulish.
Gr: Greek.
N: Norse.
OE: Old English.
S: Scots.

38. The Fenris-Wolf reminds us that all things exist in time; that there are endings as well as beginnings; but that as one thing ends, another begins at the same instant.

SELECT BIBLIOGRAPHY

Agrell, Sigurd: Lapptrumor och Runmagi. Lund, 1934.
Agrippa, Heinrich Cornelius: The fourth Book of Occult Philosophy. London, 1655.
Arbman, H.: Birka I. Stockholm, 1940.
Arntz, H.: Bibliographie der Runenkunde. Leipzig, 1937.
Aswynn, Freya: Leaves of Yggdrassil. London, 1988.
Auxentius (ed. F. Kauffmann): Aus der Schule des Wulfila. Auxentia Dorostorensis Epistola de fide vita et obitu Wulfilae. Strassburg, 1899.
Banduri, A.: Imperium Orientale. Venezia, 1729.
Björnsson, Stephán: Rimbegla. K~benhavn, 1780.
Bradley, Henry: The Goths. London, 1891.
Brion, Marcel: Théodoric roi des Ostrogoths. Paris, 1979.
Burgstaller, E.: Felsbilder in ‰osterreich. Linz, 1972.
Burns, Thomas: A History of the Ostrogoths. Bloomington, 1984.
Caillois, R.: L'homme et le Sacré. Paris, 1950.
Campbell, Joseph: Creative Mythology. New York, 1968.
Chadwick, H.M.: The Cult of Othin. London, 1899.
Chadwick, Henry: Priscillian of Avila. Oxford, 1976.
Christian, Paul (Pitois, Jean-Baptiste): Histoire de la Magie, du Monde Surnaturel et de la Fatalité ' travers les Temps et les Peuples. Paris, 1870.
Collier, Katherine P.: Cosmogonies of Our Fathers. New York, 1934.
Courcelle, P.: Histoire littéraire des grandes invasions germaniques. Paris, 1964.
Derolez, R.: Runica Manuscripta: The English Tradition. Brugge, 1954.
Dickins, B.: Runic and Heroic Poems. Cambridge, 1915.

Dornsieff, Franz: Das Alphabet in Mystik und Magie. Berlin, 1922.

Dumézil, G.: L'idéologie tripartie des Indo-Européens. Bruxelles, 1958.

Duwel, Klaus: Runenkunde. Stuttgart, 1968.

Ebers, Edith & Wollenich, Franz: Felsbilder der Alpen. Hallein, 1982.

Einarsson, S.: A History of Icelandic Literature. New York, 1957.

Elliott, Ralph W.V.: Runes: An Introduction. Manchester, 1959.

Ensslinn, W; Theodoric der Grosse. Mınchen, 1959.

Evans-Wentz, W.Y.: The Fairy Faith in Celtic Countries. London, 1911.

Ffrench, J.F.: Prehistoric Faith and Worship. London, 1912.

Gelling, Peter, & Davidson, Hilda Ellis: The Chariot of the Sun and Other Rites and Symbols of the Northern Bronze Age. London, 1969.

Gjessing, G.: Studier i norsk merovingertid. Oslo, 1934.

Grekov, B.G.: Kiev Rus. Moskva, 1959.

GrÜnbech, Vilhelm: The culture of the Teutons. London, 1931.

Hatto, A.T.: Shamanism and Epic Poetry. London, 1970.

Hauptmann, F.: Wappenkunde. Mınchen, 1914.

Heidenreich, Rob and Johannes, Heinz: Das Grabmal Theoderichs zu Ravenna. Wiesbaden, 1971.

Henning, R.: Die deutschen Runendenkmäler. Strassburg, 1889.

Herrmann, Paul: Das altgermanische Priesterwesen. Jena, 1929.

Hickes, G.: Linguarum Vett. Septentrionalium Thesaurus: 1703-1705.London, 1970.

Holmberg, Axel: Skandinaviens Hällristnigar. Stockholm, 1848.

Holmqvist, W.: Germanic Art. Stockholm, 1955.

Howard, Michael: The Runes and Other Magical Alphabets. Wellingborough, 1978.

------- -------: The wisdom of the Runes. London, 1985.

Isidorus (ed. C. Rodríguez): Historia Gothorum Wandalorum

Sueborum. Léon, 1975.

Jackson, K.H.: Language and History in Early Britain. Edinburgh, 1953.

Jansson, Sven B.: The Runes of Sweden. Stockholm, 1962.

Jones, Prudence: Eight and Nine: Sacred numbers of Sun and Moon in the Pagan North. Bar Hill, 1982.

----- ---------: Sundial and Compass Rose: Eight-fold Time Division in Northern Europe. Bar Hill, 1982.

----- ---------, and Pennick, Nigel: A History of Pagan Europe. London, 1995.

Jordanes (ed. T. Mommsen): Jordanis Romana st Getica. Berlin, 1882.

Jung, C.G.: Modern Man in Search of a Soul. New York, 1956.

Jung, Erich: Germanische Götter und Helden in christlicher Zeit. München, 1922.

Kermode, P.M.C.: Manx Crosses. London, 1907.

Krause, Wolfgang: Die Runenschriften im Alteren Futhark. Halle/Saale, 1937.

Kuhnrath, Heinrich: Amphitheatrum Aeternae Sapientiae. Hanau, 1609.

Loewe, Michael & Blacker, Carmen: Oracles and Divination. London, 1979.

MacCulloch, J.A.: The Celtic and Scandinavian Religions. London, 1948.

Marby, Friedrich Berhard: Der Weg zu den Mittern. Stuttgart, 1955.

Maxwell, J.: La Divination. Paris, 1927.

Meyer-Baer, Kathi: Music of the Spheres and the Dance of Death. Princeton, 1970.

Morganwg, Iolo (Edward Williams): The Triads of Britain, ed. Smith, Malcolm, London, 1977.

Murray, Liz & Colin: The Celtic Tree Oracle. London, 1988.

Oakshott, R.E.: The Archaeology of Weapons: Arms and Armour from Prehistory to the Age of Chivalry. London, 1960.

Osborn, Marijane & Langland, Stella: Rune Games. London, 1983.

Page, R.I.: An Introduction to English Runes. London, 1973.

Pennick, Nigel: Sacred Geometry. Wellingborough, 1980; Chieveley, 1994.

------ ------: The Subterranean Kingdom. Wellingborough, 1981.

------ ------: Die Alte Wissenschaft der Geomantie. München, 1982.

------ ------: Einst War Uns die Erde Heilig. Waldeck-Dehringhausen, 1987.

------ ------: Games of the Gods. London, 1988.

------ ------: Practical Magic in the Northern Tradition. Wellingborough,1989.

------ ------: Das Runen Orakel. München, 1990.

------ ------: Rune Magic. London, 1992.

------ ------: The Oracle of Geomancy. Chieveley, 1995.

------ ------: Runic Astrology. Chieveley, 1995.

Raphael (Smith, Robert Cross): The Philosophical Merlin. London, 1822.

Rees, Alwyn & Brinsley: Celtic Heritage. London, 1961.

Ricius, Paulus: Portæ Lucis. Augsburg, 1516.

Rutherford, Ward: The Druids. Wellingborough, 1985.

---------- -----: Shamanism. Wellingborough, 1986.

---------- -----: Celtic Mythology. Wellingborough, 1987.

Salisbury, Joyce E.: Iberian Popular Religion, 600 BC to 700 AD. New York, 1985.

Schöferdick, Knut: Der germanischer Arianismus. Misc. historiae ecclesiasticae 3 (1970), 71 - 83.

Schneider, Karl: Die germanischen Runennamen. Meisenheim, 1956.

Schütte, Gudmund: Dänisches Heidentum. Heidelberg, 1923.

Shippey, T.A.: Poems of Wisdom and Learning in Old English. Cambridge, 1976.

Shumaker, Wayne: The Occult Sciences in the Renaissance. Los Angeles, 1972.

Spiesberger, Karl: Runenmagie. Berlin, 1955.

---------- -----: Runenexerziten fır Jedermann. Freiburg-im-Breisgau, 1976.

Stanley, E.G.: The Search for Anglo-Saxon Paganism. Cambridge, 1975.

Stefansson, Vilhjalmur: Ultima Thule. London, 1942.

Stender-Petersen, A.: Varangica. Aarhus, 1953.

Stephens, George: The Old-northern Runic Monuments of Scandinavia and England. London, 1866.

Storms, G.: Anglo-Saxon Magic. Den Haag, 1948.

Sturluson, Snorri: The Prose Edda.

Syversen, Earl: Norse Runic Inscriptions. Sebastopol, California, 1979.

Taylor, I.: Greeks and Goths: A Study on the Runes. London, 1879.

Thompson, E.A.: The Visigoths in the Time of Ulfila. Oxford, 1966.

Thorsson, Edric: Futhark: A Handbook of Rune Magic. York Beach, 1984.

-------- ------: Runelore. York Beach, 1987.

-------- ------: At the Well of Wyrd. York Beach, 1988.

Tiller, Alexander: Yule and Christmas. London, 1899.

Turville-Petre, E.O.G.: The Heroic Age of Scandinavia. London, 1951.

-------- -------------: Myth and Religion of the North. London, 1964.

Verstigan, R.: A Restitution of Decayed Intelligence. Antwerpen, 1605.

von Franz, Marie-Louise: On Divination and Synchronicity. Toronto, 1980.

von Friesen, Otto: Runorna i Sverige. Uppsala, 1928.

von List, Guido: Das Geheimnis der Runen. Wien, 1912.

Wagner, N.: Getica Untersuchungen zum leben des Jordanes und zur frihen Geschichte der Goten. Berlin, 1967.

Wardle, Thorolf: Runelore. Braunschweig, 1983.

------ --------: The Runenames: Braunschweig, 1984.

Williams, Edward (editor): Barddas. Llandovery, 1862.

Wilson, David: The Vikings and their Origins: Scandinavia in the First Millennium. London, 1970.

Zeller, Otto: Der ursprung der Buchstabenschrift und das Runenalphabet. Osnabrick, 1977.

Index

Other Titles Published by Capall Bann

A detailed illustrated catalogue is available on request, SAE or International Postal Coupon appreciated. Titles are available direct from Capall Bann, post free in the UK (cheque or PO with order) or from good bookshops and specialist outlets.

Animals, Mind Body Spirit & Folklore
Angels and Goddesses - Celtic Christianity & Paganism by Michael Howard
Arthur - The Legend Unveiled by C Johnson & E Lung
Auguries and Omens - The Magical Lore of Birds by Yvonne Aburrow
Book of the Veil The by Peter Paddon
Call of the Horned Piper by Nigel Jackson
Cats' Company by Ann Walker
Celtic Lore & Druidic Ritual by Rhiannon Ryall
Compleat Vampyre - The Vampyre Shaman: Werewolves & Witchery by Nigel Jackson
Crystal Clear - A Guide to Quartz Crystal by Jennifer Dent
Earth Dance - A Year of Pagan Rituals by Jan Brodie

Earth Magic by Margaret McArthur
Enchanted Forest - The Magical Lore of Trees by Yvonne Aburrow
Healing Homes by Jennifer Dent
Herbcraft - Shamanic & Ritual Use of Herbs by Susan Lavender & Anna Franklin
In Search of Herne the Hunter by Eric Fitch
Inner Space Workbook - Developing Counselling & Magical Skills Through the Tarot
Kecks, Keddles & Kesh by Michael Bayley
Living Tarot by Ann Walker
Magical Incenses and Perfumes by Jan Brodie
Magical Lore of Animals by Yvonne Aburrow
Magical Lore of Cats by Marion Davies

Magical Lore of Herbs by Marion Davies
Masks of Misrule - The Horned God & His Cult in Europe by Nigel Jackson
Mysteries of the Runes by Michael Howard
Oracle of Geomancy by Nigel Pennick
Patchwork of Magic by Julia Day
Pathworking - A Practical Book of Guided Meditations by Pete Jennings
Pickingill Papers - The Origins of Gardnerian Wicca by Michael Howard
Psychic Animals by Dennis Bardens
Psychic Self Defence - Real Solutions by Jan Brodie
Runic Astrology by Nigel Pennick
Sacred Animals by Gordon 'The Toad' Maclellan
Sacred Grove - The Mysteries of the Forest by Yvonne Aburrow
Sacred Geometry by Nigel Pennick
Sacred Lore of Horses The by Marion Davies
Sacred Ring - Pagan Origins British Folk Festivals & Customs by Michael Howard
Secret Places of the Goddess by Philip Heselton
Talking to the Earth by Gordon Maclellan
Taming the Wolf - Full Moon Meditations by Steve Hounsome
The Goddess Year by Nigel Pennick & Helen Field
West Country Wicca by Rhiannon Ryall
Wildwood King by Philip Kane
Witches of Oz The by Matthew & Julia Phillips

Capall Bann is owned and run by people actively involved in many of the areas in which we publish. Our list is expanding rapidly so do contact us for details on the latest releases. We guarantee our mailing list will never be released to other companies or organisations.

Capall Bann Publishing, Freshfields, Chieveley, Berks, RG20 8TF.